T0312312

Cambridge Elements ☰

Elements in Ancient Philosophy
edited by
James Warren
University of Cambridge

SUSPENSION OF BELIEF

Daniel Vázquez
Mary Immaculate College

CAMBRIDGE
UNIVERSITY PRESS

Shaftesbury Road, Cambridge CB2 8EA, United Kingdom

One Liberty Plaza, 20th Floor, New York, NY 10006, USA

477 Williamstown Road, Port Melbourne, VIC 3207, Australia

314–321, 3rd Floor, Plot 3, Splendor Forum, Jasola District Centre,
New Delhi – 110025, India

103 Penang Road, #05–06/07, Visioncrest Commercial, Singapore 238467

Cambridge University Press is part of Cambridge University Press & Assessment,
a department of the University of Cambridge.

We share the University's mission to contribute to society through the pursuit of
education, learning and research at the highest international levels of excellence.

www.cambridge.org
Information on this title: www.cambridge.org/9701009500739

DOI: 10.1017/9781009028981

First published 2024

A catalogue record for this publication is available from the British Library.

ISBN 978-1-009-50073-9 Hardback
ISBN 978-1-009-01399-4 Paperback
ISSN 2631-4118 (online)
ISSN 2631-410X (print)

Suspension of Belief

Elements in Ancient Philosophy

DOI: 10.1017/9781009028981
First published online: March 2024

Daniel Vázquez
Mary Immaculate College

Author for correspondence: Daniel Vázquez, Daniel.Vazquez@mic.ul.ie

Abstract: This Element offers a systematic outline of ancient conceptions and uses of suspension of belief (understood broadly) while engaging with contemporary philosophy. It discusses the notion of *epochē* ('suspension of judgement') and other related terms, like *aporia, aphasia*, paradox, hypothesis, agnosticism, and Socratic wisdom. It examines the Academic and Pyrrhonian sceptics and some of their arguments and strategies for suspension. It also includes the use and conditions for suspension of belief in other philosophers like Socrates, Plato, Aristotle, the Stoics, Plotinus, Protagoras, and Democritus. The Element is divided into four thematic sections, each addressing one of the following questions: What is suspension of belief? When does it arise? What could its scope be? And what are its practical and moral implications?

This Element also has a video abstract: www.cambridge.org/Vázquez

Keywords: suspension of judgement, epochē, scepticism / skepticism, aporia, debate between Stoics and Academic Sceptics

ISBNs: 9781009500739 (HB), 9781009013994 (PB), 9781009028981 (OC)
ISSNs: 2631-4118 (online), 2631-410X (print)

Contents

Introduction

We get constantly bombarded with conflicting information, arguments, and opinions. People follow different principles and criteria to judge what to trust and reject. Sometimes, however, we form beliefs without sufficient grounds, and at other times we disbelieve when we ought to believe. In many cases, the decision is far from easy. These cases make us wonder if sometimes the appropriate response is to suspend our belief. But what kind of arguments or situations could lead to suspension? And what kind of epistemic attitude or state of mind is that? Is the suspension of belief a helpful stage in the search for truth? Should we always aim at getting out of it? Given the world we live in, with more information than we can process and evaluate, these are crucial questions. Today, philosophers have been engaged in lively discussions about these topics and have advanced interesting arguments and distinctions that help us find some answers. But the question and concerns are not new.

This Element offers a systematic outline of ancient conceptions and uses of suspension of belief (understood broadly) while also engaging with current discussions in epistemology and philosophy of mind. I have divided the Element into four thematic sections, each addressing one of the following questions: What is suspension of belief? When does it arise? What could its scope be? And what are its practical and moral implications?

Scholarship on suspension of belief in ancient philosophy focuses on the notion of *epochē*,[1] the two main sceptical traditions (Academic and Pyrrhonian), and their arguments and dialectical strategies. This approach often excludes closely related notions, like *aporia* ('perplexity'), *aphasia* ('non-assertion'), paradox, hypothesis, agnosticism, Socratic wisdom, and other acknowledgements of ignorance. It also overlooks the use and conditions for suspension of belief in other philosophers like Protagoras (c. 492–c. 421 BCE), Plato (429?–347 BCE), Aristotle (384–322 BCE), the Stoics, and Plotinus (204/5 – 270 CE). In these authors, we find different types of suspension of belief, not only as a result of an argument or an unsuccessful investigation but also at the beginning of the inquiry or as part of their philosophical method, including genuine and 'pretend' suspension. Here I intend to broaden the scope of the investigation to include these neglected issues and authors. As a result, I work with a more inclusive set of texts. Given my approach, I use 'suspension of belief' as an umbrella term to cover a variety of states and attitudes referred to with various Greek words and phrases.

---

[1] The term is usually translated as 'suspension of judgement'. I often leave it untranslated to distinguish it from my broader use of 'suspension of belief' as explained later, and similar terms like *aprosthetein* ('suspending judgement'), *adoxastos* ('unopinionated'), and *aklinēs* ('uncommitted').

I close my introduction with some notes for the readers. First, given that the Element's structure is thematic, it does not always follow a chronological order. However, I include all the known or approximate dates of ancient authors at their first mention. Second, I transliterate all the Greek words using the Library of Congress transliteration system for ancient Greek.[2] Third, for those unfamiliar with certain philosophical references, I have added brief explanatory footnotes to make the reading more accessible to those beginning their study of philosophy. Finally, I follow the abbreviations from the fourth edition of the *Oxford Classical Dictionary* for ancient sources and authors referred to in the footnotes.[3]

1 What Is Suspension of Belief?

1.1 Contemporary Analysis and Ancient Echoes

What do we mean when we say we suspend our belief? There is a fruitful debate among current philosophers about how to answer this question. Here I offer a broad and incomplete landscape of the recent discussion and distinctions in use. My goal is twofold. First, to show how contemporary authors have tried to map the concept of suspension, and how it is a lively theoretical puzzle. Second, to use these recent accounts and distinctions as a starting point to help us compare, understand, and analyse ancient texts when appropriate, without imposing them on the ancient texts, but reflecting on their similarities and differences. Additionally, it will help me show that some contemporary accounts have ancient antecedents beyond Pyrrhonian scepticism – the only ancient philosophy explicitly mentioned in these discussions – and that current analyses do not exhaust what we find in ancient accounts.

Let me first consider the distinction between suspension and mere lack of belief. According to Friedman (2013b, 165–170), when we suspend our belief, it seems we do it regarding something we are inquiring into or intend to judge. So, no one suspends their belief about something they disregard or are entirely ignorant of. Thus, we cannot describe suspension just as the joint absence of belief and disbelief about *p* or as an absence of belief about *p* and belief about non-*p* because we would fail at distinguishing suspension from mere lack of belief.

Moreover – Friedman continues – suspension is not opting out, giving up, or simply quitting a deliberation. We can do all that for all sorts of practical reasons without suspending our beliefs. So, for example, when someone is discussing reproductive rights and the time for the debate runs out, the tone becomes

---

[2] Accessible at www.loc.gov/catdir/cpso/romanization/greek.pdf.

[3] List is accessible at https://oxfordre.com/classics/page/3993. The only exception is Diogenes Laertius' *Lives and Opinions of Eminent Philosophers*, abbreviated as DL.

uncivil, or the parties are not listening to each other, people might decide to quit the conversation. That would not imply anyone has conceded or suspended their belief.

These initial distinctions are clear enough. But the concept of suspension of belief may still prove difficult to pin down. Philosophers today disagree on how to understand suspension of belief across various aspects.

To better approach the state of the question, let me distinguish between judgement and belief. McGrath (2021, 7) puts it this way: 'to judge that p is to *make up* your mind that p, whereas to believe that p is to have your mind *made up* that p'.[4] Notice that belief does not entail judgement. We believe many things, form new beliefs, or lose them without judging them. I hold ordinary beliefs I acquired unreflectively just by living and interacting with others. And I acquire new beliefs all the time. For example, I look out the window and see a squirrel in my garden. So, I form a belief about it. When I forget things completely, I lose my beliefs without having to judge them. They simply slip from my mind. Do I have any meetings next week? I have no clue. Simply forgetting something does not imply suspension.

In contrast, when I judge something, I form a belief by making up my mind about it. And if I suspend that judgement, the point is to refrain from belief itself. So, when philosophers talk about suspension of judgement, they are interested not only in suspending judgement but in the resulting suspension of belief.[5] Yet, philosophers characterise suspension of judgement differently and disagree on whether there are various species of suspension and whether we can reduce other types of neutral attitudes or states of mind to it.

Masny (2020, 5010), for example, distinguishes three dimensions in which recent views on this topic differ: (1) whether suspension is reducible to beliefs and desires; (2) whether the relevant attitudes have first-order or higher-order content (i.e., whether suspension is about facts about the world or about our beliefs and desires about the world)[6]; and (3) whether those attitudes are directed to propositions or questions.

Modern philosophers, Masny argues, have defended four different combinations (see Table 1). Some people support a reductive, first-order content, proposition-directed attitude account. This means that suspension of judgement is reducible to beliefs and facts about them. Wedgwood (2002), for example, writes: 'one "suspends judgment" about p when one consciously considers p,

---

[4] This account assumes the orthodox view that disbelief is fundamentally the same attitude as belief, only differentiated by its negative content. But see Lord (2020, n. 1).

[5] See McGrath (2021, 7–8), who warns us of exceptions like irrationality, fragmented minds, and non-belief-forming judgements. But, for the most part, I will not discuss those exceptions here. For irrationality, see Section 2.2.

[6] Friedman (2013c, 180) calls them higher-order accounts, and Crawford (2004) metacognitive accounts.

Table 1 Accounts of suspension according to Masny (2020).

Structure	Content	Direction	Authors
Reductive	First-order	Proposition-directed	Salmon, Wedgwood, Sturgeon, Moon
Non-reductive	First-order	Proposition-directed	Atkins
Non-reductive	First-order	Question-directed	Friedman
Reductive	Higher-order	Proposition-directed	Russell, Crawford, Masny

but neither believes nor disbelieves p. (To "consider" p is just to "entertain" p; it is for p to 'occur' to one in occurrent thinking.)'.[7] For Atkins (2017), however, suspension is a sui generis first-order propositional attitude. Suspending, for him, cannot be explained with a combination of beliefs, disbeliefs, or other basic propositional attitudes. Thus, his view is a non-reductive, first-order content, proposition-directed attitude. Friedman (2013c, 2017) also considers suspension a sui generis attitude. She argues it is 'an attitude that expresses or represents or just is one's neutrality or indecision about which of p, $\neg p$ is true'.[8] However, for her, suspension is directed towards questions, not propositions. It is an interrogative attitude, which entails inquiring into the question subject to suspension of judgement.[9] Thus, hers is a non-reductive, first-order content, question-directed attitude account. Finally, Russell (1953), Crawford (2004), and Masny (2020, 5010) argue for a reductive, higher-order content, proposition-directed interpretation, where suspension involves beliefs about our epistemic position. Masny's account is a good example of this group. He calls his view 'Crawford Plus', which describes suspension in the following way:

> S suspends judgement about p iff (i) S believes that she neither believes nor disbelieves that p, (ii) S neither believes nor disbelieves that p, (iii) S intends to judge that p or not-p.[10]

This is still an incomplete picture. DePaul (2004), for example, rejects the attitudinal approach altogether, and others represent suspension and other non-committal attitudes with middling or imprecise credences, that is, the level of confidence we have on a proposition in an interval between 0 and 1 or with degrees of belief.[11]

---

[7] Masny also puts here Salmon (1986, 1989), Sturgeon (2010), and Moon (2018).
[8] Friedman (2013c, 180). [9] Friedman (2017).
[10] See Masny (2020, 5024). See also Raleigh (2021).
[11] For agnosticism, see van Fraassen (1998), Hájek (1998), Monton (1998), Sturgeon (2010), and Friedman (2013b). For a general discussion, see Lord (2020). On the relation between belief and credence, see Jackson (2020).

Another point of contention concerns whether suspension is the attitude or reaction one always has or ought to have when faced with specific reasons (like a balance of evidence) or whether one has direct voluntary control over which beliefs get suspended.[12] Notice, however, that two aspects need to be distinguished here. One is the description of suspension of belief as a psychological datum, that is, when it happens regardless of being a rational or irrational reaction (including rashness, failure of understanding and disregarding evidence). The other is the normative account of suspension, which explains when it is rational to suspend judgement and when not, and when it is permissible to do it for other reasons (e.g., for practical or methodological motivations).

I will not adjudicate between all these recent accounts here. What I find interesting is that some of their features are evocative of how ancient authors explain or represent suspension of belief. For example, it seems that higher-order content, proposition-directed accounts of suspension have a similar structure to Socratic wisdom and *aporia,* as described in some of Plato's dialogues and other sources (see Section 1.3.1). Moreover, Friedman's account explicitly attempts to capture something close to, or at least a version of, Sextus Empiricus' Pyrrhonian *epochē*.[13] At the same time, scholars disagree on how to interpret charitably Sextus' *epochē*: as the description of an involuntary reaction (a psychological datum) or as a rational normative account.[14]

The modern discussion has also led to distinctions with parallels in scholarship in ancient authors. In response to Friedman's account, some insist that there are not one but two types of suspension. Wagner (2021), for instance, distinguishes between inquiry-opening suspension and inquiry-ending suspension. Similarly, Staffel (2019) argues that suspension serves as either a transitional or a terminal attitude in our reasoning. These proposals mirror discussions regarding the interpretation of *epochē* in Sextus. Some see two different types of *epochē*: one that arises during the process of inquiry and another that is a final and static state.[15]

---

[12] See Friedman (2013a, 155) Lord (2020), Masny (2020, 5013), and Section 2.

[13] Sextus Empiricus is the most influential of the ancient Greek sceptics. He flourished during the mid-late 2nd century CE, and we preserve three of his works: *Outlines of Pyrrhonism* (*Pyrrhōneioi hypotypōseis*), *Against the Professors* (*Adversus Mathematicos* 1-6; the word *mathematicos* here means 'learned' and includes many disciplines), and a text transmitted as the last part of *Against the Professors* (*Adversus Mathematicos* 7-11) but now recognised as an independent but incomplete work sometimes referred to as *Adversus Dogmaticos*. For other attempts at capturing Sextus' *epochē* or accounts inspired by his scepticism, see McGrath (2021), Grgić (2014), and Wieland (2014). Since Aenesidemus (1st century BCE) and Sextus take inspiration from Pyrrho, their form of scepticism is often called Pyrrhonian scepticism.

[14] See Barnes (1990), Vázquez (2009, 2019, 2021), Perin (2015), and Sections 1.1.2, 2.2, and 4.1.

[15] See Vázquez (2009), Bullock (2016), and Section 1.2.

Instead of proposing different types of suspension, some authors distinguish between different neutral stances. Friedman (2013c) uses suspended judgement and agnosticism as synonyms, but others consider them two different states. Wagner (2021), for example, understands agnosticism as a complex mental state that involves not only suspension but also a commitment to the indecision derived from suspension (thus, agnosticism entails suspension, but not vice versa). In turn, McGrath (2021, 9) understands agnosticism as an intermediate state of confidence, whereas Lord (2020) thinks of agnosticism as an anti-interrogative attitude. The idea that suspension of judgement and agnosticism might be different states could help us understand the difference between certain interpretations of Academic and Pyrrhonian scepticism, between Protagoras' religious agnosticism, some of Plato's claims, and Sextus Empiricus' religious scepticism. Finally, we could compare the contemporary typology with sceptical and methodological uses of suspension.

For now, though, I turn to the ancient author most famously associated with suspension: Sextus Empiricus. He offers the most explicit and detailed account of suspension of belief in antiquity. His texts also open the door for looking at his antecedents and other ways of expressing neutrality, which I outline in Section 1.3.

1.2 Suspension in Sextus Empiricus

According to Sextus, the sceptics are inquirers who 'began to do philosophy to decide among appearances and apprehend which are true and which are false' (*PH* 1.26).[16] They assumed that by doing philosophy in this way, they would find *ataraxia* ('peace of mind', 'tranquillity'). However, instead of discovering the truths and the understanding they sought, sceptics found all sorts of disputes whose opposing sides seemed equally convincing. This equipollence or equal strength of the matters under investigation makes it impossible to decide which side of the dispute is correct, so they suspended judgement (*PH* 1.196). And when they did, *ataraxia* followed fortuitously (*PH* 1.26).

Sextus uses the Greek verb *epechein*, which means 'to suspend', 'to stop', or 'to withhold'. This suspending of judgement has a punctual beginning prompted by the inability to decide. When Sextus elaborates on what he means by it, he simply identifies it with being unable to say which option is convincing and which one is not:

> We use 'I suspend judgement (*epechō*)' for 'I cannot say (*ouk egō eipein*) which of the things proposed I should find convincing and which I should not find convincing', making clear that objects appear to us equal in respect of

─────────────
[16] All transl. Annas & Barnes (2000), modified.

convincingness and lack of convincingness. Whether they are equal, we do not affirm: we say what appears to us about them, when they make an impression on us. (*PH* 1.196)

The phrase 'I suspend judgement' reports an inability to assert, not a voluntary act of withholding (I come back to this in Section 2.2). In this regard, Sextus' suspending is unlike Cartesian doubt, which is a systematic and voluntary exercise in doubting the truth of one's own beliefs (Section 2.1.2). Notice also that Sextus suspends judgement only when he finds equipollence in respect of convincingness or lack of it. This equipollence is an appearance that strikes people individually. What seems equipollent to one person might not seem equipollent to another. The language is reminiscent of the modern notion of middling credences or confidence mentioned in the previous Section. However, Sextus never talks about degrees, assigned values, or thresholds of credibility or confidence. Still, Sextus' suspending seems to grow out of equipollence in an analogous way some epistemologists think coarse epistemic attitudes (belief, disbelief, and suspended judgement) grow out from real-valued credences.

Often, however, Sextus describes the sceptic already in a state of mind he calls *epochē,* which is the nominalisation of *epechein* and is traditionally translated as 'suspension of judgement'. He describes it as 'a standstill of the intellect, owing to which the sceptic neither rejects nor posits anything' (*PH* 1.10). This state consists of a feeling of settled indecision or neutrality that results from the inquiry: 'The sceptical lifestyle (*agōgē*), then, is also called [. . .] suspensive (*ephektikos*), from the feeling (*pathos*) that comes about in the inquirer *after* the investigation' (*PH* 1.7). Once the sceptic is in *epochē,* this state of mind explains why the sceptic does not assert or deny anything, and not vice versa.[17] Sextus also uses *aphasia* to refer to this state of mind. This identification between *epochē* and *aphasia* becomes clear at *PH* 1.192, where Sextus writes that '*aphasia* is the feeling (*pathos*) we have because of which we say that we neither posit nor reject anything'.

Epochē (or *aphasia*), however, does not assume that the investigation is over, nor does it entail an anti-interrogative attitude. On the contrary, for Sextus, the sceptical lifestyle is also investigative (*zētētikos, PH* 1.7), and the sceptics are the only ones still investigating the truth (*PH* 1.3). Thus, *epochē* might be a settled indecision, and although it does not require active investigating, it leaves the questions open. It does not imply a dogmatic commitment to indecision or the anti-interrogative attitudes suggested by

---

[17] Compare the distinction between *epechō* and *epochē* with Friedman's (2013c, 179) 'suspend*ing* judgement' and 'suspend*ed* judgment'.

some contemporary definitions of agnosticism.[18] However, it is unclear whether the investigative attitude stems from *epochē* or is an additional sceptical attitude compatible with it.

Most interpreters conceive *epochē* as the passive outcome of an unresolved inquiry. First, I ponder whether *p*. Then, I discover I cannot make up my mind whether *p* or not-*p*. As a result, my mind falls into a passive state of indecision. However, this description is slightly inaccurate because it confuses involuntariness and stillness with passivity.

On the one hand, the sceptic does not choose *epochē*; she falls into it. It happens to the sceptic, like other involuntary attitudes (e.g., liking, dislike, or disdain), and unlike a set of attitudes and beliefs we can voluntarily adopt or reject (e.g., supporting abortion rights or boycotting a company). Here I will call the involuntary attitudes and feelings 'postures', and the voluntary attitudes 'stances'.[19] But the involuntariness of *epochē* does not entail a general passivity. When I am undecided about what to order from a restaurant's menu, I actively try to decide, even if I am involuntarily at a standstill, incapable of doing it. I am far from being in a passive state. I am trying hard to decide. When I ask the waiter for two more minutes, I still ponder the situation, even when I interrupt the process to resume my conversation with my dinner partners.

Consider Dr Seuss's (1957) *How the Grinch Stole Christmas!* After failing to ruin the holiday, the Grinch watches the Whos still singing without presents. He 'stood puzzling and puzzling: How *could* it be so?' and 'puzzled three hours, till his puzzler was sore'. He stood still at the top of the mountain on a cold winter morning, but every second he was in an intense intellectual endeavour. The same happens with Buridan's Ass. I imagine the animal paralysed, but its mind actively considering between the stack of hay and the pail of water.[20] Being in *epochē* cannot be a completely passive state or forgetting about the topic. It is, at least, to have the question in the back of your mind, still open.

Perhaps for this reason, Sextus tells us that the sceptical lifestyle is also called aporetic (*aporētikos*) 'either (as some say) from the fact that it puzzles over (*aporein*) and investigates everything, or else from its being at a loss (*amēchanein*) whether to assent or deny' (*PH* 1.7). Sextus uses the term

---

[18] See Wagner (2021) and Lord (2020).

[19] See van Frassen (2004), Lipton (2004), Teller (2004) and Cassam (2019, chap. 4).

[20] Buridan's Ass is a hypothetical scenario in which a donkey (an ass), equally hungry and thirsty, stands at an equal distance between a stack of hay and a pail of water. Since it cannot decide what to do, the donkey dies of inanition. The name refers and satirises the moral determinism of Jean Buridan (c.1301–c.1359/62).

aporetic in two senses: one refers to actively puzzling over a question, whereas the other refers to being at a loss as to what to say. The latter fits with *epochē* as the state of mind after the investigation. The former refers to the fact that when we inquire and have not yet made up our minds, we might be in suspension, but we are also intellectually active.[21] This suspension that occurs during the investigation seems also captured in Sextus' clarification of the phrase 'I determine nothing' (*ouden horizō*):

> When Sceptics say, 'I determine nothing', what they say is this: 'I now feel (*pepontha*) in such a way as neither to posit dogmatically nor to reject any of the things falling under this investigation'. When they say this, they are saying what is apparent to them about the subject proposed – not dogmatically making a confident assertion but describing and reporting how they feel (*paschei*). (*PH* 1.197)[22]

Like the passages about *epochē* and *aphasia*, this quote emphasises that Sceptics' neutrality is not voluntary but a feeling they report to have. But in 'I determine nothing', the feeling could result (notice the perfect tense in *pepontha*) from developments in an ongoing investigation, not just after it has ended.

There is another interesting side to this phrase. Sextus is aware that using it could be construed as a dogmatic assertion. For this reason, he explains that the sceptic determines nothing, meaning not assenting to unclear objects, 'not even "I determine nothing" itself' (*PH* 1.197). In this way, Sextus uses a semantic paradox to escape the charge of dogmatism: to assent to 'I determine nothing', the sceptic must not assent to it. Sextus compares this use of sceptical expressions to other famous paradoxes, like 'Everything is false' and 'Nothing is true'.[23] These phrases cancel themselves[24] in such a way that uttering them cannot be said to entail belief (*PH* 1.14). Sextus compares them with the effect

---

[21] For different readings of the aporetic label, see Woodruff (1988, 142) and Castagnoli (2018, 207). For the distinction between *epochē* and Platonic *aporia*, see Woodruff (1986, 27–28). In DL 9.70, we are told that followers of Pyrrho are also called Aporetics. Sextus acknowledges that Arcesilaus' philosophy is aporetic (*PH* 1.232-234), and Photius reports that for Aenesidemus, the Pyrrhonists 'are both aporetic and free from all doctrine' (*Bibl.* 169b40-41; in LS71C6). For Aenesidemus see Section 3.2.

[22] Annas and Barnes' translation follow Heintz reading *ou dogmatikōs . . ., all' apangeltikōs*. For the Academics' take on this phrase, see Section 3.2.

[23] Sextus attributes 'everything is false' to Xeniades of Corinth (c.450-c.345 BCE; see *Math.* 7.53-54, 388; *PH* 2.18, 76; DL 6.30-1, 36, 74, 82) and a similar thesis, 'everything is bullshit [or "an illusion"]' (*typhon ta panta*), to the cynic Monimus (4th century BCE; *Math.* 8.5; but cf. DL 6.83). For discussion, see Brunschwig (2017). The second phrase, 'nothing is true', reminds us of Democritus (c.460–c.356 or 380 BCE; Ar. *Metaph.* Γ 1009b9-12), Aristotle's discussions in *Metaph.* Γ (1007b26 and 1012b24-25), Pyrrho (c.360–c. 270 BCE; DL 9.61), and Aenesidemus (*Math.* 8.40). On the last two, see Sections 1.3.3-4 and 3.2.

[24] See *heautēn symperigraphei* (*PH* 1.14), *heautō perigraphesthai* (*PH* 1.15), and *heauton symperigraphein* (*Math.* 8.480). For a detailed discussion of these terms in Sextus, see Castagnoli (2000).

of purgatives: 'just as purgative drugs do not merely drain the humours from the body but drive themselves out too along with the humours' (*PH* 1.206). In a different place, he adds that self-cancelling things 'put themselves in the same conditions they put other things. For example, just as fire after consuming the wood destroys itself as well' (*Math.* 8.480).[25]

It is unclear, however, what these last passages entail for our interpretation of *epochē*. Sextus is often loose in using terms, and his professed attitude is not to fight over words (*PH* 1.207). In the past, I have proposed that two different types of *epochē* may be at play, one active and one passive.[26] But the notion of *epochē* may not exhaust the epistemic neutrality of the sceptic, and maybe we should distinguish between *aporein*, *epechō*, and *epochē*. For my purposes, it suffices to say that Sextus' sophisticated description of suspension of belief opens the door to look for its antecedents and other ancient approaches to suspension of belief in a broad sense. In the following section, I briefly describe and compare how some of Sextus' predecessors conceive and write about suspension of belief and closely connected attitudes and states.

1.3 Suspension before Sextus

The term *epochē* was probably introduced by Pyrrho or Arcesilaus (315/4–241/40 BCE)[27] and is used mainly by Hellenistic authors. However, previous philosophers discussed neutral postures and stances using different terms and phrases. Some authors use *aporia*, *aporein* and formulations reminiscent of Sextus' account of *aphasia* and related expressions. There is also a long tradition of philosophers interested in paradoxes, ignorance, Socratic wisdom, and refutation, which often lead to retracting claims or withholding assent. How did philosophers conceive of these notions, and what did they think of their relationship? How do these notions relate to suspension of belief? I cannot offer an exhaustive analysis, but I shall mention some highlights. First, I discuss acknowledgements of ignorance, Socratic wisdom, and some paradoxes associated with similar views. Then, I track down the uses of *aphasia* and *aporia*. I briefly mention lack of opinions and commitments in Pyrrho, and I finish with the notions of *epochē* and belief in the debate between Academic sceptics and Stoics.

1.3.1 Socratic Wisdom and Paradoxes

A natural way to signal epistemic neutrality is to acknowledge one's ignorance. Consider, for example, Protagoras' religious agnosticism when he claims about

---

[25] Transl. Bett (2005).   [26] Vázquez (2009).

[27] DL 9.61 credits Pyrrho with the introduction of *epochē*, but at 4.28, credits Arcesilaus. See Couissin (1929).

the gods, 'I cannot know (*ouk echō eidenai*) whether they exist or whether they do not'.[28] Similarly, when someone asks me which candidate will win the next election, I reply that I don't know. In my case, it means that I have not made up my mind about it. I could be interested in knowing, aware of the options and recent polls, and still fail to form a belief. Maybe public preferences are shifting, and it is difficult to predict who will come on top. Protagoras' case might be a more committed agnosticism, though. He could have considered the matter and concluded that he would never be able to form a belief about the subject or refuse to inquire because he has good reasons to think he will not succeed.

Some philosophers distinguish between opinion and knowledge. In such cases, someone could claim no knowledge of a subject yet hold all sorts of opinions about it. Take Xenophanes, who suggests that in religious matters, the fallback position is opinion, not suspension.[29] However, Protagoras seems to mean that he not only holds no knowledge but also no opinions about the existence of the gods. Similarly, when I acknowledge my ignorance about who will win the election, what I mean is that I have no knowledge or opinion about it, despite inquiring and being interested in the question.

Expressing one's ignorance is not the most precise way to convey a neutral stance or posture. As we saw, mere lack of belief is not suspension (Section 1.1). But in many communicative contexts, if someone discloses ignorance, it is often safe to infer that what they mean is suspension of belief.[30] But what would we need to be more explicit and precise? As I showed, some modern philosophers understand suspension as higher-order beliefs or knowledge of ignorance, plus some additional conditions. To use Masny's (2020, 5024) definition again, maybe I could say I believe that this year I neither believe nor disbelieve that Barcelona will win the Champions League, I neither believe nor disbelieve it, but I intend to judge it before the end of the season. We seem to find examples of neutrality expressed in analogous ways in ancient philosophy.

Socrates (469–399 BCE) is famously known for saying that 'he knew nothing except the fact that he knew nothing' (DL 2.32). On its own, this claim sounds like disclosure of a general, almost global, neutral stance. Such an interpretation might go as far back as Arcesilaus, the first sceptical Head of the Academy. Or at least to Cicero (106–43 BCE), when he reports that 'Arcesilaus used to deny

---

[28] Euseb. *Prep. evang.* 14.3.7. See also DL 9.51, Cic. *Nat D.* 1.24.63, and Philostr. *VS* 1.10.1-4. For a different interpretation of the fragment, see Kerferd (1981, 165–168). For recent discussion see Henry (2022).

[29] Sext. Emp. *Math.* 7.49; DL 9.72 (1-2); Plut. *De audiendis poetis* 17e-f (1-2)=DK21B34.

[30] The technical term for this is 'conversational implicature', which is implying one thing (pragmatic meaning) by saying something else (semantic meaning); see Davis (2024).

that anything could be known, not even the residual claim Socrates had allowed himself, i.e., the knowledge that he didn't know anything' (*Acad.* 1.45).[31]

Socrates' famous claim, however, is nowhere to be found in Plato or any of the other early sources. The closest we get is Plato's *Apology* 21d. When Socrates discovers that those who appear wise were not, he thought to himself:

> I am wiser than this man; it is likely that neither of us knows anything worthwhile, but he thinks he knows something when he does not, whereas when I do not know, neither do I think I know; so I am likely to be wiser than he to this small extent, that I do not think I know what I do not know.[32]

In this passage, the scope of Socratic ignorance, the force of the claim and its formulation differ from the claim found in Diogenes Laertius and Cicero. For Plato, the extent of Socrates' ignorance is not absolute but restricted to what is worthwhile (*kalon kagathon*; lit. 'beautiful and good'). Socrates might have some other types of knowledge, and he does not entirely rule out the possibility of having some worthwhile knowledge. Moreover, Plato's Socrates does not claim to have *knowledge* of his ignorance. He only claims that he does not think to know what he ignores (although he considers himself wiser than others because of that).[33]

The difference between these Socratic claims is not trivial. But both cases seem to convey not mere lack of knowledge but something akin to suspension of belief.[34] Given that Socrates was engaged in a philosophical inquiry into the topics he claims to be ignorant of, his position falls closer to higher-order content conceptions of suspension. We might be tempted to construe Plato's Socrates as saying that he does not believe (nor disbelieve) that he knows what he ignores and does not know what he ignores but intends to judge it.

If generalised, this type of higher-order content formulation risks becoming paradoxical. For example, when I say I know that I know nothing. If it is true, then I do know something, which makes what I said false. But the claim cannot be both true and false. Someone might worry that these paradoxical formulations are self-defeating nonsense. But as mentioned in the previous section, Sextus Empiricus, at least, embraces them and says that the sceptics can use

---

[31] All transl. Brittan (2006). On Arcesilaus see Sections 1.3.4, 3.2.1, and 4.1.

[32] Transl. Grube in Cooper & Hutchinson (1997).

[33] On Socrates' epistemic superiority, see Woolf (2008).

[34] See also *Hp. mi.* 272a6-c7, where Socrates claims he knows nothing. His ignorance is the product of holding an opinion, discovering that the wise has an opposite opinion, and blaming himself for being worthless and mistaken, but willing to learn. See also Arist. *Soph. el.* 34.183b6-8. Xenophon (c. 430–355 or 354 BCE), however, actively tries to counter this image of Socrates (*Mem.* 4.4.9-12). See Natali (2008).

them precisely because these expressions are self-cancelling, which protects the sceptic against any accusation of affirming or denying them, even if using them alienates the sceptic's interlocutors.

A formulation like the one Cicero attributes to Arcesilaus (nothing can be known) could be accused of the same problem. However, since it is not a knowledge claim, Arcesilaus avoids paradox.[35] Cicero attributes a similar but more extreme version of this statement to Metrodorus of Chios (fl. 4th century BCE), who 'claimed at the beginning of his book *On Nature*: I declare that we don't know whether we know anything or nothing, not even whether we know that or not, or altogether whether anything is the case or not' (Cic. *Acad.* 2.73).[36] Metrodorus' formulation also seems designed to be as general as possible while avoiding contradiction or paradox (more on this in Section 3). But is the implication mere ignorance or suspension?[37]

1.3.2 Aphasia *and* Aporia

We find the term *aphasia* already in Euripides (c. 480–c. 406 BCE), meaning speechlessness caused by surprise or fear (*Hel.* 549 and *Heracl.* 515). In Plato, we find it only twice. Both instances report a certain incapacity to respond to an argument. The first is in *Philebus*. After listening to Socrates, Protarchus says: 'this argument has left me absolutely speechless (*aphasian pantapasi*) for the moment' (21d4). The second is in the *Laws* (636e), where Megillus confesses that he and his companions cannot say anything (*aphasia*) to respond to the Athenian's arguments. Although using other terms or phrases, we find confessions like this in many other dialogues. Like the previous ones, most happen when someone cannot refute or contest an argument.[38] Sometimes, *aphasia* occurs after *aporia*.

At its core, *aporia* is a distinctive way of being puzzled or perplexed due to an inquiry into a difficult philosophical question. It is an intellectual impasse in which we perceive no way out or lack the resources to answer a question we have been discussing. Speechlessness or incapacity to articulate thoughts is

---

[35] Assessing Cicero's report is difficult. See Brittain & Osorio (2021a). Some sources attribute similar claims to Democritus: 'In reality we know nothing: for truth is in the depths' (DL 9.72=DK68B117; transl. Graham (2010)) and to Empedocles: 'everything is hidden, that we sense nothing, discern nothing, and that we can't discover what anything at all is like' (Cic. *Acad.* 2.14). I return to Arcesilaus in Section 1.3.4. For the scope of Academic *epochē*, and whether it is self-defeating, see Section 3.2.1.

[36] See also DL 9.58, and Democritus' acknowledgement of ignorance in Section 2.1.1.

[37] For a study of the fragment, see Brunschwig (1996, 32–37).

[38] See, e.g., 'I have nothing to say' (*Cri.* 54d8), 'trapped in the end and have nothing to say' (*Resp.* 6.487c1-2), 'I have nothing left to say' (*Lysis* 222e7), and 'I, Crito, lay speechless' (*Euthyd.* 303a4-5). Transl. Cooper & Hutchinson (1997). See also *Phd.* 107a2-7.

a frequent effect.[39] This philosophical use of the term *aporia* goes back to the everyday use of the word *aporos*, which means 'impassable', 'pathless', 'without means or resources', and 'at a loss'[40] Heraclitus (fl. c. 500 BCE) uses it in this way when he says, 'If one does not expect the unexpected one will not find it (*exeurein*), for it cannot be searched out (*anexereunēton*) nor arrived at (*aporon*)'.[41]

We can also trace back *aporia* to the reception of Xenophanes (c.570–c.478 BCE) and Zeno of Elea (c.495–c.430 BCE). In one report, we read, 'Xenophanes was in *aporia* about all things and held as his only dogmatic view that all things are one and that this is god, who is limited, rational, and changeless' (Ps-Gal. *Hist. phil.* 7=DK21A35).[42] The contrast between *aporia* and holding dogmatic views suggests that the former entails suspension of belief.[43]

Aristotle, in turn, reports that 'Zeno was puzzled (*ēporei*) because if place is something, it will be in something' (*Ph.* 210b22-25).[44] We get the following explanation of the puzzle in Simplicius. 'For every existing thing ought to be somewhere. But if place is an existing thing, where could it be? Surely in another place, and that in turn in another and so on indefinitely' (*In Phys.* 563.17–20, Eudemus fr. 78). Therefore, we are invited to infer that place does not exist. But how does that lead to *aporia* instead of, for example, a *reductio ad absurdum*? It causes *aporia* if someone, for example, is neither completely ready to reject the argument nor give up the belief that place must exist. The normative recommendation might be to suspend belief, but the discomfort of such a fallback position propels the inquiry forward. Maybe it does not even require us to suspend our belief about the existence of place, but only about whether we can explain why that is the case.

The obvious place to study the use of *aporia* is Plato's dialogues. Plato offers different, seemingly inconsistent accounts of *aporia*. He often describes it as a passive state of mind. Meno, for example, famously describes it as having

---

[39] See *Lach.* 194b, *Meno* 80a-b, *Phlb.* 21d, *Soph.* 247b-c, and cf. *Chrm.* 168a-169c. My understanding of *aporia* is indebted to Politis & Karamanolis (2018). See also Woodruff (1988, 141).

[40] The question that produces perplexity is also called *aporia*. Politis and Karamanolis (2018, 2) distinguish two senses of *aporia*: the subjective (being perplexed) and objective use (a two-sided question that produces perplexity). In this section, I focus on the subjective use.

[41] Clem. Al. *Strom.* II, 17=DK22B18, transl. Laks & Most (2016). See Palmer (2018).

[42] Transl. Laks & Most (2016).

[43] Xenophanes' exact epistemological position is difficult to determine. According to some texts, he thought that certain type of knowledge is out of our reach. Still, he seems to assume that the fallback position is belief, not suspension, although it is unclear whether that is a descriptive or a normative claim. See fr. 35 (Sext. Emp. *Math.* 7.49, 110, 8.326; DL 9.72, 1-2; Plut. *Quomodo adul.* 17e-f, 1-2=DK21B34), and Ar. Did. *In Stob.* 2.1.17=DK21A24.

[44] Translations by Graham (2010). See also *Ph.* 209a23–25, Simpl. *In Phys.* 562.3-6=DK29B5, and Eudem. fr. 42 *apud* Simpl. *In Phys.* 563.25–28 (all testimonia in DK29A24).

touched a torpedo fish and getting one's mind and tongue numb (*Meno* 80a-b). In *Laches*, Socrates describes *aporia* as being storm-tossed by an argument (194c). But other passages suggest a more active picture. In the *Meno*, Socrates claims to be more perplexed than anyone else about what virtue is, but his perplexity makes him keep the enquiry going.[45] Later, he stresses that *aporia* fosters a desire to find the correct answer to the question under discussion (*Meno* 84b-c).[46] This suggests that Socrates conceives *aporia* as an active cognitive process consisting of puzzling over a question to find the answer. But then, which is it? Is it a passive perplexity or a restless mulling over a question? The answer is both.

The Platonic images offer, on the one hand, a descriptive illustration and, on the other, a normative account of *aporia*. Secondary interlocutors like Meno and Laches provide descriptive illustrations: a window into how some people react to *aporia*. They show a spectrum of possible reactions to perplexity caused by argument. Some people get upset or frustrated or assume their interlocutor has harmed them. For example, after failing to answer what courage is, Laches acknowledges *aphasia* and frustration: 'I am really getting annoyed at being unable to express what I think in this fashion' (*Lach.* 194a8-b1). But Laches's *aphasia* does not entail suspension: 'I still think I know what courage is, but I can't understand how it has escaped me just now, so that I can't pin it down in words and say what it is' (*Lach.* 194b1-4). Unlike Plato's Socrates (and the Sceptics), Laches disconnects his puzzlement and speech-lessness from his claim of knowledge. Thus, he claims to know even if he cannot articulate it in words. If knowledge is not connected to explanation, Laches's position is rational. But if we accept, with Plato's Socrates, that knowledge is necessarily linked to explanation, then Laches's position is irrational (see Section 2.2).

In contrast, Plato's Socrates provides a normative account. He explains what we ought to do when we find ourselves in *aporia*. In other words, he is interested in the epistemically responsible thing to do. When someone is receptive to *aporia*, it marks cognitive progress in the investigation. It lets you become aware of your ignorance and mistakes, inviting you to withhold or withdraw judgement and keep looking.[47] In other words, if in *aporia*, you should suspend belief. These beneficial features of *aporia* also help distinguish it from the puzzlement derived from eristic argumentation. The difference, however, is not so much in the puzzling itself but, as Jan Szaif (2018, 41) remarks, in 'the *ethos* underlying the refutational practice'. Eristic argumentation aims to

---

[45] Socrates could be insincere about his puzzlement but that would be morally problematic, uncooperative, and unnecessary.

[46] See also *Resp.* 524a6–b5 and 524e2–5a2.   [47] See Szaif (2018).

entertain, impress, and defeat interlocutors.[48] Instead, aporetic philosophical elenchus seeks to find the truth and acquire knowledge, or at least avoid erroneously claiming to know what one does not know. Could the difference be in the persistent intention to judge the issue?

Aporia is an important concept in philosophy after Plato, too. We find it in Arcesilaus, Aenesidemus, Aristotle, Plutarch (c.45–120 CE), Sextus Empiricus, Alexander of Aphrodisias (fl. late 2nd and early 3rd centuries CE), and other later thinkers.[49] Here I cannot discuss the whole evolution of the term, but I shall return to some of these authors in later sections. For now, it suffices to say that philosophers used *aporia* as a philosophical tool and assumed that the problems that cause this type of puzzlement must be resolved to make up our minds about the questions under discussion.

1.3.3 Lack of Opinion in Pyrrho

Pyrrho (c.360–270 BCE) wrote nothing and what we know from him comes from different sources. His thought appears influenced by Democritus[50] and Anaxarchus (c.380–320 BCE).[51] Some people think that he had contact with Indian philosophy.[52] In one of the surviving reports, we get the following argument from his disciple, Timon (c.320–230 BCE):

> [a] According to Timon, Pyrrho declared that things are equally undifferentiated/ undifferentiable (*adiaphora*), unstable/unmeasurable (*astathmēta*) and indeter- minate/indeterminable (*anepikrita*). [b] For this reason (*dia touto*), neither our sensations nor our opinions tell the truth or lie. [c] Therefore, for this reason we must not trust them, but we should be unopinionated (*adoxastos*), uncommitted (*aklinēs*) and unwavering (*akradantos*), saying concerning each individual thing that it no more is than is not, or it both is and is not, or it neither is nor is not. [d] The outcome for those who actually adopt this attitude, says Timon, will be first speechlessness (*aphasia*), and then freedom from disturbances (*ataraxia*). (Aristocles *ap.* Euseb. *Praep. evang.* 14.18.2–4=LS1F3-5; Caizzi 53)[53]

The interpretation of this passage is the epicentre of heated debate. One of the sources of disagreement is how to read the adjectives *adiaphora*, *astathmēta*, and *anepikrita*. Are they characterising reality or our epistemic limitations to access

---

[48] See de Souza & Vázquez (2019).   [49] See Karamanolis & Politis (2018).

[50] See DL 9.30-49=DK68A1, Simpl. *in Phys.* 28.15=DK68A38, and Sext. Emp. *Math.* 7.135=DK68B9.

[51] Ps.-Gal. *Hist. Phil.* 7=DK72A15.

[52] See DL 9.61. Pyrrho and Anaxarchus may have taken part in Alexander the Great's expeditions in 334 BCE, where they could have met and learnt from Indian magi or early Buddhist masters. The extent of the influence is contested. See, e.g., Flintoff (1980), Hankinson (1995, 58–65), Chiesara (2004, 28–29), and Beckwith (2015).

[53] Transl. Long & Sedley (1987). See also DL 9.65=LS3C; Caizzi 60.

it? We could read the Greek terms in both ways. Depending on how we take them, the first claim [a] is either metaphysical, epistemological or both.[54] Many also take issue with the second sentence [b]. Stopper (1983, 293), for example, complains that the inference from [a] to [b] looks 'zany', and it should go the other way around. He suggests, following Zeller (1909, 501), amending the text from *dia touto* ('for this reason') to *dia to* ('on the grounds that'). In this way, the unreliability of our sensations and opinions would explain that the things are *adiaphora, astathmēta,* and *anepikrita,* not vice versa. This change would place Pyrrho closer to what later sceptics argue. However, his suspension would be derived from the nature of our epistemic faculties, not from equipollence.[55] According to this, we can reconstruct the main argument in at least two ways:

Version 1
1. If things are undifferentiated, unstable, and indeterminate, our sensations and opinions do not tell the truth or lie [implicit].
2. Things are undifferentiated, unstable, and indeterminate [a].
3. Therefore, our sensations and opinions do not tell the truth or lie [b] (from 1&2).
4. If premise 3 is the case, we should not trust our faculties but be unopinionated, uncommitted, and unwavering [implicit].
5. Therefore, we should not trust our faculties but be unopinionated, uncommitted, and unwavering [c] (from 3&4).[56]

Version 2
1'. If our sensations and opinions do not tell the truth or lie, things are undifferentiable, unmeasurable, and indeterminable [implicit].
2'. Our sensations and opinions do not tell us the truth or lie [b'].
3'. Therefore, things are undifferentiable, unmeasurable, and indeterminable [a'] (from 1'&2').
4'. If premise 3' is the case, we should not trust our faculties but be unopinionated, uncommitted, and unwavering [implicit].
5'. Therefore, we should not trust our faculties but be unopinionated, uncommitted, and unwavering [c] (from 3&4).

---

[54] Scholars use this claim to argue that Pyrrho is either a metaphysical dogmatist, a sceptic, or an agnostic about the world outside appearances. For the first group see Burnyeat (1980), Decleva Caizzi (1981), Long & Sedley (1987), Bett (1994, 2000, 2002), Hankinson (1995), Chiesara (2004), Brunschwig (1994), Lesses (2002), and Thorsrud (2009). For sceptical readings, see Patrick (1929), Stough (1969), Long (1974), Stopper (1983), Annas & Barnes (1985, 10–14), Groarke (1990), Brennan (1998), and Green (2017). A hybrid interpretation in Svavarsson (2004).

[55] See Green (2017). Regarding claim [b], Brunschwig (1994) argues we should not attribute it to Pyrrho but to Timon. There is also disagreement on how to interpret *alētheuein* ('tell the truth') in [a]. See Section 4.1.

[56] For criticisms on this reconstruction, see Green (2017, 24–27).

I will not adjudicate here which interpretation is correct. I only want to highlight that the normative recommendation is a suspension of belief in both cases. And the neutral stance results from voluntarily withholding or retracting belief. That is why when we perceive something or ponder an opinion, we should remind ourselves that it no more is than is not, or it both is and is not, or it neither is nor is not.[57] Given the metaphysical indeterminacy of sensible things, our cognitive limitations, or a combination of both, the rational thing to do, Pyrrho suggests, is to remain *adoxastos* and *aklinēs*. So, we ought to get rid of all our beliefs.[58] Moreover, notice that suspension follows from the argument and that *aphasia* follows suspension, not vice versa, as in Sextus Empiricus. The evidence is insufficient, but it is tempting to construe both versions of Pyrrho's argument as higher-order accounts akin to a settled agnosticism instead of an active and inquiring suspension.

1.3.4 The Debate between Stoics and Academic Sceptics

This debate goes back to the Platonic Academy under the headship of Polemo (c.350–267 BCE) and Crates (died c.268–264 BCE). Polemo taught both Zeno of Citium (c.334–262 BCE),[59] the founder of Stoicism, and Arcesilaus, who became the head of the Academy after Crates and began what is known as the New or Sceptical Academy, which focused on arguing dialectically, cross-examining other philosophical traditions, without revealing their own views.[60] The evidence suggests that the interchange between Zeno and Arcesilaus was civil and focused on the characterisation of Stoic wisdom and the Stoic sage, specifically, on what the sage can know and the practical implications of answering that question.[61] Later, the debate became a complex and lengthy interchange between the Stoics and Academics. I will only mention some aspects relevant to our topic.[62]

According to the Stoics, our souls receive different types of impressions or presentations (*phantasiai*) from the world around us, which affect us by revealing themselves and their causes (DL 7.49–51; Aëtius 4.12.1–5). We can evaluate

---

[57] Cf. Arist. *Metaph.* Γ.4, 1008a31-34, and 1008b21-25. See Hankinson (1995, 94) and Chiesara (2004, 25). In DL 9.76=LS1G (Caizzi 54), Timon explains that the phrase *ou mallon* ('no more this than that') means 'to determine nothing, but suspend judgement (*aprosthetein*)'. On *aprosthetein*, a hapax, see Long & Sedley (1987, vol. 2, 7).

[58] However, Brunschwig (1994, 207–208) thinks *pragmata* ('things') includes only the practical and ethical sphere.

[59] DL 7.2 and Cic. *Acad.* 1.34 (Varro).

[60] For possible exceptions see discussion later, and Sections 3.2.1-2, and 4.1.

[61] See Cic. *Acad.* 2.76-77 and *Acad.* 1.34; Plut. *Mor.* I.4.11 (*Quomodo adulator ab amico internoscatur*) 55c. Scholars sometimes frame the debate as purely epistemological. But the notion of wisdom at the core of the debate has significant ethical implications. See Snyder (2018).

[62] See Salles & Boeri (2014, chaps. 6–7).

these impressions to either accept or reject them. For example, when I open my bedroom window, I receive the impression that it is daytime. I usually accept this impression as true and form the belief that it is in fact daytime. The Stoics distinguished, however, between different types of assents to impressions. Sometimes, they thought, assent is firm and secure; other times, however, it is given to false or non-cognitive impressions, hastily or in a weaker form than required. In these latter cases, they think we have no knowledge but only opinions.[63]

The Stoics held that only the sage has true knowledge, virtue, tranquillity, and happiness. Moreover, they argued sages are infallible, and their assent to the impressions would always be stable, unimpeded, and perfectly free. And given the way they conceive opinions, the sage must be unopinionated. To guarantee this rather demanding image of the sage, the Stoics held that a sage would only assent to what they call 'cognitive impressions' (*phantasiai katalēptikai*). These were special kinds of impressions, but the translation might be misleading. The Greek word *katalēpsis* means 'grasping', but one of Cicero's ways of referring to it in Latin was *cognitio*, where we get the Standard English translation (*Acad.* 2.17).[64] However, its difference with other impressions is not that they have to do with cognition as we understand the term now, but that they were obviously true, precise, cannot be or become false, and are the basis for knowledge.[65] The way they put it was to say that cognitive impressions arise from 'what is', formed in such a way that they could not have come from 'what is not', and are so patently true that are their own guarantee; they do not require further justification beyond themselves and, thus, can be the foundation for our knowledge.[66]

The Academics granted (perhaps only for the sake of the argument) that the sages should not assent hastily but challenged the existence of cognitive impressions. Then, they argued that the Stoic sage would have to suspend judgement on all matters:

> They [i.e., the Academics] confront the Stoics with appearances. In the case of things which are similar in shape but different objectively it is impossible to distinguish the cognitive impression from that which is false and incognitive. E.g. if I give the Stoic first one and then another of two exactly similar eggs to discriminate, will the wise man, by focusing on them, be able to say infallibly that the one egg he is being shown is this one rather than that one? The same argument applies in the case of twins. For the virtuous man will get

---

[63] Sext. Emp. *Math.* 7.151-7 and Plut. *De stoic. rep.* 1056E-F. See Vázquez (2020).

[64] Cicero also uses *perceptio* ('perception', 'comprehension') and *comprehensio* ('apprehension').

[65] See Adamson (2015, 62).

[66] DL 7.46-7, 7.54; Sext. Emp. *Math.* 7.247-260, 7.151-157, 7.415-421; Nemesius *apud* Euseb. *Praep. evang.* 14.6.13. See Sellars (2006, 68–69).

a false impression, albeit one from what is and imprinted and stamped exactly in accordance with what is, if the impression he gets from Castor is one of Polydeuces. (Sext. Emp. *Math.* 7.408–10=LS40H4)[67]

For the Academics, if the Stoics cannot show that there are cognitive impressions, then their normative fallback position should be *epochē*. In other words, they should have no opinions and make no claims of knowledge.

In this dialectical context, Cicero reports: 'Arcesilaus used to deny that anything could be known [. . .] He thought that everything was hidden so deeply and that nothing could be discerned or understood. For these reasons, he thought we shouldn't assert or affirm anything, or approve it with assent: we should always curb our rashness and restrain ourselves from any slip' (Cic. *Acad. post.* 1.45; LS68A1, part).[68] It is not easy to know whether Arcesilaus was committed to these views. But, at least in some sources, he seems to hold to an epistemological theory in which suspension is the normative outcome of the arguments (I return to this point in Section 3.2.1).

The Stoics responded in various ways to the Academics, but here I will mention only one reply, illustrated in the aforementioned report about the Stoic Sphaerus (c.285 BC–c.210 BCE):[69]

> Once, when a discussion arose about whether the sage will form opinions, Sphaerus said that they would not. The king wanted to refute him and ordered wax pomegranates to be set out. Sphaerus was fooled and the king shouted that he had assented to a false presentation, to which Sphaerus nimbly replied by saying that what he had assented to was not that they were pomegranates but that it was reasonable that they were pomegranates. There was a difference between a cognitive impression and a reasonable (*eulogon*) one. (DL 7.177=LS40F1-2)[70]

The king presents Sphaerus with an indiscernibility challenge analogous to the Stoic objection using a realistic wax pomegranate. But how are we supposed to understand the story? Scholars have offered two readings. One is to think that Sphaerus concedes he assented to a reasonable impression instead of a cognitive

---

[67] Transl. Long & Sedley (1987). See also Cic. *Acad.* 2.40, 54–58, and 83–86; Sext. Emp. *Math.* 7.247-260=LS40E, K, and 7.415-42=LS37F. Polydeuces is an alternative name for Pollux. A different line of attack was to compare alleged cognitive impressions with false impressions while dreaming, in a fit of madness, or drunk (Cic. *Acad.* 2.47-53, 2.88-90, Sext. Emp. *Math.* 7.402-408).

[68] Transl. Brittan (2006). Cf. Cic. *Acad.* 2.66-67, 77. See also Sext. Emp. *PH* 1.232-3, *Math.* 7.155-7.

[69] For other responses, see Cic. *Acad.* 2.20, 50, 51-58.

[70] Transl. Inwood (2008), modified. In a slightly different version of the story, we get a final explanation: 'The former, i.e. the cognitive impression, is incapable of deceiving, but the reasonable impression can turn otherwise' (Athenaeus 354E=LS40F3). Cf. Arcesilaus' use of the reasonable (*to eulogon*) in Section 4.1.

one, as the last sentence suggests. That would mean that Sphaerus had an opinion: he assented to something that could turn out false. But this does not necessarily mean the king has refuted Sphaerus. Sphaerus could still answer that the king mistakenly considered him a sage when he never claimed to be one.[71] Later Stoics are quick to acknowledge they are not sages, so it is possible that Sphaerus would take a similar approach.[72] A different reading assumes that Sphaerus considers himself a sage but argues that he assented to the cognitive impression 'it is reasonable that this is a pomegranate', which was true. In this case, the king's challenge fails because it has not shown that the Stoic sage has any opinion.[73] Maybe a combination of these two readings is correct: Sphaerus did not consider himself a sage, and he assented to a cognitive impression.

The debate over the existence of cognitive impressions and the possibility of universal *epochē* was kept alive by subsequent generations of Stoics and Academics. But by the time the Academy was under the headship of Philo of Larissa (159/8–84/3 BCE), the Academics had started to argue for more restricted forms of *epochē*. Perhaps they were still arguing only dialectically. However, Aenesidemus, who may have studied with Philo, famously described the debate of his time as 'Stoics fighting with Stoics'.[74]

I will come back to this debate later (Sections 3.2.1 and 3.2.2), but here I want to highlight that we can see two different ways of conceiving suspension of belief. On the one hand, the Stoic sage arrives at suspension of all beliefs without suspending all their judgements. This is possible because, for the Stoics, opinion is a weak assent to what is false or non-cognitive,[75] which the sage avoids by only assenting to cognitive impressions and thus acquiring infallible knowledge, not mere beliefs. On the other hand, the Academic sceptics remain unpersuaded of the existence of cognitive impressions and claims of knowledge, arguing for universal *epochē*, even if they are not endorsing the argument or allow weak, pragmatic, or residual commitments to some claims, as I shall show in Sections 3 and 4.

2 When Does Suspension of Belief Arise?

Depending on how one describes it, suspension of belief could arise rationally, irrationally, or non-rationally. If we agree that we ought to behave rationally, certain circumstances might call for suspending our beliefs as

---

[71] See Ioppolo (1986, 83–85).   [72] Sen. *Ep.* 116; *Ep.* 59, 13-14.

[73] See Brennan (1996, 2000, 166–167).

[74] Phot. *Bibl.* 170a16=LS71C9. The dates and Aenesidemus' involvement in the Academy have been disputed by Caizzi (1992) and Mansfeld (1995).

[75] Sext. Emp. *Math.* 7.156 (in LS41C), Cic. *Acad.* 2.59=LS69F and Plut. *De stoic. rep.* 1056E-F=LS41E.

the appropriate normative recommendation (expressed under the form 'you should/ought to suspend belief over *x*').[76] For example, when our criteria for either belief or disbelief are not met, suspension is the rational position to take until something changes. Call this rational suspension. But, of course, we often fail to live up to our standards of rationality. We sometimes keep believing when we should not, or we withhold belief even in the face of decisive evidence. When we do things like that, we behave irrationally from an epistemic point of view.[77] Taking a neutral stance in this way is what I call an irrational suspension. Finally, suspension may be a response that does not depend on following or transgressing any normative commitment or rationality rule but a particular psychological and affective state that happens involuntarily. In that case, suspension is not a stance we can adopt or reject but a non-rational posture.[78]

I discuss two groups of ancient texts that deal with rational suspension. The first deals with cases where we ought to suspend belief because we discover a balance of evidence and we do not want to hold incompatible beliefs (Section 2.1.1). The second case is not a situation in which we ought to suspend our beliefs but in which it is permissible to do so for methodological reasons, that is, not because it follows logically from our epistemic commitments but because it promises to help us reach some insight or the truth about a given topic, or because it is the best we have (Section 2.1.2). Finally, I discuss whether we have ancient texts dealing with irrational and non-rational suspension (Section 2.2).

2.1 Rational Suspension

In some ancient sceptical texts, the threshold for belief formation or possession is significantly high. The arguments suggest that we should only form a belief if we meet strict conditions; otherwise, we should suspend our beliefs. Consider,

---

[76] This could be described as a commitment to one or more requirements of rationality or normative principles of rationality. In scholarship on Pyrrhonian scepticism, the discussion often focuses on whether the sceptic is committed to these requirements or principles. See Barnes (1990, 21), Fogelin (1994, 114–116), Harte & Lane (1999), Lammenranta (2008), Perin (2010), and Vázquez (2019).

[77] There are many non-epistemic reasons to suspend belief: pragmatic convenience, peer pressure, and fear of hurting someone's feelings. Suspending for these reasons would be rational in a broader sense, but here I use rational in the sense of following the epistemically responsible attitude towards a belief (i.e., concerning whether we can reasonably determine if a belief is true or not).

[78] Nowadays, many epistemologists assume or defend 'doxastic involuntarism', the idea that we do not have voluntary control over our beliefs because we cannot believe at will. However, see Roeber (2019). In ancient authors, the common assumption is that we have voluntary control over our beliefs, even if we do not have it over impressions and appearances.

for example, Aenesidemus' first mode for the suspension of judgement.[79] This mode argues that our perceptions are unreliable for belief formation because other animals' perceptions differ from ours. And there is no way to prefer our perceptions over theirs, even if we try to supply proof that this is acceptable (*PH* 1.60–61).[80] For the sceptic, this mode leads to equipollence and suspension. And although the argument is not devoid of merit, one might complain that it is too demanding, and sets the threshold for belief artificially high.

For other philosophers, the threshold for belief formation is low because they consider belief a fallible epistemic state that falls short of knowledge, as in Plato and Aristotle,[81] or an undesirable state to be avoided altogether, as it is for the Stoics.[82] In all these cases, suspension could sometimes arise as the fallback position when belief or knowledge formation fails or when we have reasons to abandon a belief but not enough reasons to disbelieve it entirely. But under which conditions does this happen? Most cases fall into a balance of evidence.

2.1.1 Balance of Evidence

Many philosophers suppose or argue that we ought to suspend our belief when there is a balance of evidence on the question under investigation. I understand 'balance of evidence' in a broad sense, including cases where one is confronted with two equally good arguments or comparable empirical observations, and also when there are two equally bad arguments, or the arguments or questions are muddled in such a way that they cause utter confusion. Similarly, insufficient, or total lack of evidence could balance the scales in a way that leave suspension of belief as the only rational alternative.

Ancient philosophers often used a balance of evidence to argue for suspension of belief. Consider Aenesidemus' ten modes. Each of them points to different contexts in which appearances conflict. The second mode 'concerns

---

[79] Pyrrhonian sceptics often talk about 'modes' instead of arguments for *epochē* (but see Sext. Emp. *PH* 1.36). The Greek word is *tropos* ('turn', 'direction', 'way', 'mode') from the verb *trepō* ('to turn'). They are devices used to guide people into *epochē* (Sext. Emp. *PH* 1.31). The Pyrrhonian sceptics use different lists of modes, and the one known as the 'ten modes' is traditionally attributed to Aenesidemus. However, Aristocles (Euseb. *Praep. ev.* 14.18.11) only attributes him nine. For other reservations on the attribution, see Hankinson (1995, 109–110).

[80] Cf. DL 9.80.

[81] See Pl. *Resp.* 5, and Ar. *An. Post.* I, 33. See also Epiph. *Adv. haeres.* 3.2.9=DK70A23, where we are told that Metrodorus of Chios complained that no one knows anything because the things we believe we know we do not strictly know; for everything is by belief.

[82] The Atomists also deny that we have genuine knowledge and do not seem to allow reasonable belief (Epiph. *Adv. haeres.* 3.3.9=DK67A33).

the various natures of men and their idiosyncrasies. [...] one man has a passion for medicine, another for farming, and another for commerce. And the same things harm some men and benefit others. Hence one must suspend judgment' (DL 9.80–81).[83] If someone asks what the good life is, Aenesidemus will point at various pieces of conflicting evidence. If the outcome is a balance of evidence, or, as he calls it, an equipollence (*isostheneia*; lit. 'of equal strength') where competing possibilities are equally persuasive, the only rational answer will be suspending our beliefs.[84] Annas and Barnes (1985, 24–25) explain the general structure of these arguments like this:

(1) x appears F in S
(2) x appears F^* in S^* (where F and F^* designate incompatible properties, while S and S^* designate different situations)
but the appearances are equipollent, i.e.
(3) we cannot prefer S to S^* or vice versa
Hence we arrive at suspension of judgement, i.e
(4) we can neither affirm or deny that x is really F or really F^*

This type of argument has a long tradition. Academic sceptics used them too.[85] They oppose sense perceptions, conceptions, arguments, ideologies, and cultural practices, among other things. But the opposition of perceptions and arguments goes back at least as far as Protagoras.[86] He claims that 'it is possible to argue every position pro and con with equal plausibility –including the very question whether every position can be argued pro and con' (Sen. *Ep.* 88.43).[87] This thesis, however, does not lead him to suspend his beliefs. Instead, he maintains his famous 'man measure' doctrine: 'Of all things the measure is man, of the things that are that they are, of the things that are not that they are not' (Sext. Emp. *Math.* 7.60, Pl. *Tht.* 152b2-3=DK80B1).[88] Plato, Aristotle, and Sextus took this to mean that all opinions and judgements are as they appear to each individual, so that each one of us is the ultimate authority on one's own judgements. This was complemented by Protagoras' claim that all opinions are true (for each believer) and that contradicting anyone is impossible.[89] Since this interpretation faces some objections, some scholars have interpreted Protagoras not as a relativist but as a pluralist, a perspectivist

---

[83] Transl. Mensch (2018), modified.   [84] Assuming the principle of non-contradiction.

[85] See Cic. *Acad.* 1.45-46; *Acad.* 2.42, 79; and DL 4.28.

[86] See Fr. 2 (Didymus the Blind, *On the Psalms* pt. 3, p. 380 Gronewald 222.20-25).

[87] Transl. Graham (2010). See also DL 9.50-56=DK80A1.

[88] Cf. Sext. Emp. *PH* 1.216-19=DK80A14.

[89] DL 9.51. and Pl. *Euthyd.* 286b8-c4=DK80A19. On how Protagoras' epistemology relates to his agnosticism, see Henry (2022). See Pl. *Tht.* 162e2. The idea that contradiction is impossible is attributed to Antisthenes (c.446–366 BCE) too (Ar. *Top.* 1.11, 104b19-20).

or a pragmatist,[90] but my point here remains. For him, the opposition of arguments does not necessarily lead to suspension of belief.

Democritus also opposes perceptions to cast doubt on their reliability:[91]

> [M]any of the other animals have appearances contrary to ours concerning the same things, and even for each one of us, relative to himself, the same things do not always seem the same to perception. Which, then, of these appearances is true or false is unclear (*adēlon*). For the one lot is no more true than the other lot, but rather equally so. That is why Democritus, at any rate, says that either there is no truth or that to us at least it is unclear (*adēlon*). (Ar. *Metaph.* Γ.5, 1009b7-12=DK68A112)[92]

Democritus' argument concludes with a disjunctive: either there is no truth in appearances, or it is unclear to us (he uses the term *adēlon*, which means 'unclear', 'unknown', or 'obscure').[93] When I perceive that the apple in front of me is red, either that has no truth value,[94] or, if it has, it is unclear to me whether it is true or false, given that others perceive the same object differently. Either way, it seems that I should not rush my judgement. Could Democritus' position defend a neutral stance regarding our sense perceptions? It seems so, although it is difficult to be sure.

According to Sextus, Democritus considered the senses a 'bastard' or 'obscure' (*skotios*) kind of cognition. Although he is clear that they cannot be a source of knowledge only of opinion, he also recognises that knowledge begins with the senses. In other texts, Democritus claims that perceptual properties are relative and dependent on agreement: 'By convention colour, by convention sweet, by convention bitter, but in reality atoms and void.'[95] So, it is unclear if he thinks we should dismiss or withhold from forming sensory judgements or simply acknowledge their relative and conventional status.[96]

---

[90] See Bonazzi (2021).

[91] But compare with Anaxagoras Fr. 22 (Sext. Emp. *Math.* 7.90=DK59B21).

[92] Transl. Reeve (2016). See also Ar. *Gen. corr.* 315b6-15=DK67A9. Cf. *Metaph.* K.6, 1063a35-b7.

[93] See also DL 9.72=DK68B117: 'In reality we know nothing; for truth is in the depths'. Transl. Graham (2010). This acknowledgement of ignorance does not seem unrestricted (cf. Section 1.3.1) since elsewhere he argues that reality is made from imperceptible atoms and void. Other texts offer a qualified version of the claim: 'In reality we understand nothing *securely*, but we perceive what changes in relation to the disposition of the body as things enter or resist'. And: 'That in reality we do not now understand what the nature of each thing is <or> is not, has been made evident in many ways'. Sext. *Math.* 7.136 (in DK68B9). Cf. Pl. *Ph.* 65b.

[94] Or it is false, depending on how we read 'there is no truth'.

[95] Gal. *Galeni de elementis ex Hippocrate libri ii*, 1.2 (Kühn 1.417=DK68A49). Trad. Graham (2010).

[96] See Sext. Emp. *Math.* 7.135 (in DK68B9=B125); Gal. *De experientia medica* 15.7=DK68B125; Aetius [P 4.9.8] S 1.50.24=DK67A32, and Sext. Emp. *Math.* 7.138-139=DK68B11.

Moreover, in other places, Aristotle attributes to Democritus the thesis that truth lies in appearances,[97] which some find difficult to reconcile with sense perception scepticism. Despite these tensions, it might be possible to fit together Democritus' claims. If he thought that suspension of belief follows when we consider our sense perceptions alone, that would be compatible with thinking that they are a necessary requirement for knowledge or that they contribute to knowledge when supplied with other sources of information.[98]

In Plato's *Protagoras* (360d8–362a4) we find another interesting case. After conversing for a while, Socrates tells Protagoras that the discussion has turned against them. As if it had a voice on its own, it mocks them both for changing sides. As a result, matters stand now 'terribly confused' (*tarattomena deinōs;* 361c3). Socrates is willing to continue investigating, but Protagoras uses the conundrum to exit the conversation, promising to revisit the topic at another time. Socrates' fallback position seems to be suspension of belief.[99]

Another possible case of suspension due to unclarity is the Stoic response to the sorites paradox. The paradox is generated by asking to specify a clear boundary between vague terms like bald, few and many: 'Chrysippus thinks that when one is asked to specify gradually whether, for example, three things are few or many one should come to rest (*hēsuchazein,* as they put it) a little before one reaches "many"' (Cic. *Acad.* 2.93=SVF 2.277). According to Cicero, the recommendation cannot simply be to stop answering but must also include withholding assent.[100]

As mentioned earlier, Academic sceptics also used balance of evidence to advocate for suspension of belief. Arcesilaus would ask his interlocutors to state and defend their opinions while he would argue against them (Cic. *Fin.* 2.2). This is how Cicero describes Arcesilaus' dialectical method: 'by arguing against everyone's opinions he drew most people away from their own, so that when reasons of equal weight were found on opposite sides on the same subject, the easiest course was to withhold assent from either side' (*Acad.* 1.45).[101] Later, Arcesilaus' successor as head of the Academy, Carneades (214–129/8 BCE), would become famous for arguing both sides of a case or

---

[97] Ar. *De. an.* I.2 404a27-31; *Gen. corr.* I.2 315b9=DK67A9.

[98] I cannot do justice to this complex topic here, but for some examples of the different interpretations of Democritus' epistemology, see Lee (2005, chaps. 8–9), Curd (2001), Morel (1996), Taylor (1999, 216–222), and Barnes (1979).

[99] In other cases, Plato's Socrates does not suspend belief but describes a constant vacillation of beliefs (*Ph.* 96a6-b8).

[100] Cic. *Acad.* 2.94. But see Zinke (2021) who construes these cases differently.

[101] See also Cic. *Fin.* 5.10.

question.[102] According to some sources, he was sent by Athens as an ambassador to Rome, where he gave a series of lectures on justice, scandalously arguing in its favour one day and against it the next morning.[103]

These cases use a balance of evidence either to reach suspension of belief or to conclude that perceptual knowledge is impossible. But for Aristotle, recognising that there is a balance of evidence in certain topics is just the beginning of the philosophical inquiry. In *Topics* 1.11 (104b3-5), he describes dialectical problems as a point of contention where people 'either have no opinion, or the public think the opposite of the wise, or the wise think the opposite of the public, or each of these groups has opposed opinions within itself'.[104] He later explains that there are also dialectical problems of which 'there are contrary deductions (for there is a puzzle whether it is so or not, because there are persuasive arguments about both sides), as well as those about which, because they are vast, we have no arguments' (*Top.* 104b12-15).

However, Aristotle thinks that we ought not to inquire into every problem, but only those which cause us to be at a loss (*aporeō*), *and* we can solve by argument (*Top.* 105a3-9).[105] Aristotle does not *say* we should suspend belief when we find a balance of evidence. But he thinks that if we are genuinely puzzled, we should examine all sides of the question to make up our minds about it.

In *Nicomachean Ethics* 9.8, for example, when discussing 'whether a person should love himself or someone else most of all' (1168a28-29),[106] Aristotle writes: 'It is quite natural that there is a puzzle (*aporeitai*) about which view we should follow since both are plausible; presumably, then, we should separate arguments like this from one another and determine how far and in what way those on each side are true' (1168b10-12).[107] These are two views about how to lead one's life, and without determining which one to follow, we are either stuck, like Buridan's Ass, or else behaving epistemically irresponsibly.

In *Metaphysics* B, Aristotle incorporates the *aporiai*[108] and the examination of the competing arguments to answer them as a required first part of the inquiry that leaves us in a better position to make a judgement:

---

[102] This follows the Socratic practice in early Platonic dialogues of setting two-sided difficulties (*aporiai* in the objective sense distinguished in footnote 40). See Politis (2018).

[103] Lactant. *Div. inst.* 5.14.3-5 and *Epit.* 50.8, which summarise the now-lost Cicero's *De republica* (3.9-11). See also Quint. *Inst.* 12.1.35, and Jer. *Ep.* 50.2.1. However, see Powell (2013), who doubts the details and historicity of Carneades' lectures. See Sections 3.2.1–2.

[104] All transl. Smith (1997).   [105] I come back to this passage in Section 3.3.

[106] All transl. Crisp (2000).   [107] See also Arist. *Eth. Eud.* 7.1-2, 1235a4-b18.

[108] The questions that produce perplexity (the objective use of *aporia*; see footnote 40).

It is necessary, with a view to the science we are inquiring into, first to go
over topics about which we should first raise puzzles (*aporēsai*). These
include both topics about which people have supposed divergent things,
as well as any separate from these that may have been overlooked. Now
for those who wish to be puzzle-free (*euporēsai*) it is useful to go through
the puzzles (*diaporēsai*) well. For the subsequent puzzle-free (*euporia*)
condition is reached by untying the knots produced by the puzzles raised
in advance, and it is not possible to untie a knot you are unaware of. But
a puzzle (*aporia*) in thought makes clear the existence of a knot in the
subject matter. For insofar as thought is puzzled (*aporei*) it is like people
who are tied up, since in both cases it is impossible to move forward. That
is why we must get a theoretical grasp on all the difficulties beforehand,
both for these reasons and because those who inquire without first going
through the puzzles (*diaporēsai*) are like people who do not know where
they have to go. And, in addition, a person [who has not already grasped
the puzzles] does not even know whether he has found what he is inquiring
into. (*Metaph.* B.1, 995a24-995b1)[109]

Notice that Aristotle's first step is to raise the puzzles, even if he presupposes
that we can solve them with the appropriate analysis. But for a puzzle to be
such, all sides must appear convincing and generate an initial impasse.[110]
Moreover, the puzzles might reveal the objective complexity of an issue under
investigation.

Aristotle recognises that being aware of a puzzle or genuinely puzzled
about an issue might not be enough to move the inquiry forward. So, he adds
a conditional: 'for those who wish to be puzzle-free it is useful to go through
the puzzles well'. Otherwise, one might opt for committed neutrality or
disregard the puzzle.[111] But Aristotle sides with those who wish to be
puzzle-free. At the same time, he recognises that without a balance of
evidence there is no puzzle; we would simply select the side with the
stronger argument or evidence.

Plotinus employs a similar method, setting up *aporiai* and trying to solve
them (*Enn.* I.1). But he explicitly acknowledges that some *aporiai* might not
have a solution. He argues that in cases like the *aporiai* about the soul, even if
we do not find a solution, we might benefit from the enquiry by finding out what
in this area does not admit of solution:

Concerning the soul, the right course, I feel, would be to conduct our
enquiry in such a way as either to arrive at solutions to the relevant
problems, or, if remaining in a state of puzzlement (*aporos*) on those

---

[109] All transl. Reeve (2016).   [110] See also Arist. *Top.* 101a35-36.
[111] Some aspects of Aristotle's methodology are reminiscent of those of Sextus Empiricus. See
Long (2006, chap. 3).

points, to regard this at least as a gain, that we know what in this area does not admit of solution. On what subject, after all, would one more reasonably spend one's time in prolonged discussion and investigation than on this one? (*Enn.* IV.3 [27] 1.1–6)[112]

Dillon and Blumenthal (2015, 166) comment on this passage, 'It is notable, and typical of Plotinus' approach to philosophy, that he should recognize that the honest admission that some problems may not admit of solution is a valid conclusion of philosophical investigation.' This suggests that Plotinus is open to the possibility of agnosticism in some topics: a committed neutral stance that results from the negative results of an inquiry. We can understand this knowledge as follows:

> *S* knows that the question of whether *p* or not-*p* does not admit solution iff (a) *S* has inquired (i.e., has had prolonged discussion and investigation) about it, and (b) *S* remains in *aporia*.

Indeed, this does not necessarily close the door to further investigation and changing one's mind about the question. But it explains one's claim of knowledge and sets a higher threshold for engaging in further inquiry.

Suspension of belief also follows when there is little or no evidence, which we can also see as a balance of (lack of) support on both sides of the question. In this case, there is no support, or the evidence is insufficient to decide which side is better. On the question whether the number of stars is odd or even, we have nothing at all to help us choose between one or the other.[113] And as for little evidence, consider again Protagoras' religious agnosticism. The full fragment reads as follows: 'Concerning the gods, I cannot know whether they exist or whether they do not, or what form they have; for there are many obstacles to knowing, including the obscurity (*adēlotēs*) of the question and the brevity of human life.'[114] One way of reading the passage is this: nothing people say about the gods counts as sufficient evidence for or against the existence and nature of the gods, or at least not at first glance. But adjudicating all the views would take too long for a human being to sort out, so Protagoras prefers to suspend his belief and remain neutral.[115]

---

[112] Transl. Dillon & Blumenthal (2015).

[113] Sext. Emp. *PH* 2.91, 97, 231; *M* 7.393, 8.147, 317; Cic. *Acad.* 2.32; Epict. *Diss.* 1.28.3.

[114] Euseb. *Prep. evang.* 14.3.7; DL 9.51=DK80B4. Transl. Graham (2010). See also Hesychius from a scholium on Plato *Republic* 600c (DK80A3), and Cicero, *Nat. D.* 1.24.63.

[115] Scholars disagree on the exact scope, force and meaning of Protagoras' assertion. Is the focus on him not knowing whether the gods exist or on the fact that the obstacles to knowing apply to all human beings? Could his declaration signal crypto-atheism? See, e.g., Gagarin (2002), Mansfeld (2018), and Whitmarsh (2015, 87–91).

In Plato's *Statesman*, we find another passage where the lack of historical records or information about a topic leads the main character, the Eleatic Stranger, to suspension of belief. The context is the cosmological myth, where the Eleatic Stranger narrates that before current humans, there was another race guided by minor gods and living a life without toils. The question is whether they had a more blessed life than us. The Eleatic Stranger thinks humans are not well equipped to answer this question:

> Well then, if, with so much leisure available to them, and so much opportunity to get together in conversation not only with human beings but also with animals – if the nurslings of Cronus used all these advantages to do philosophy, [. . .], the judgment is easy, that those who lived then were far, far more fortunate than those who live now. But if they spent their time gorging themselves with food and drink and exchanging stories with each other and with the animals of the sort that even now are told about them, this too, if I may reveal how it seems to me, at least, is a matter that is easily judged. But however that may be, let us leave it to one side, until such time as someone appears who is qualified to inform us in which of these two ways the desires of men of that time were directed in relation to the different varieties of knowledge and the need for talk. (*Pol.* 272b1-d4)[116]

The Eleatic Stranger's proposal to leave the question to one side results from not having adequate sources. Notice that there is no *aporia*, no genuine philosophical puzzle. The question would be easily judged if they had access to relevant factual evidence or reliable witnesses. Plato uses the Greek verb *aphiēmi* (*Pol.* 272d2), which means 'to give up', 'let go' and 'put away'. The rational recommendation is to stop discussing the topic because both options seem equally reasonable in the current context.

2.1.2 Methodological Suspension and Hypothetical Reasoning

Suspension of belief can be part of a philosophical method in multiple ways. In some cases, reaching a genuine suspension due to the refutation of our ideas might be crucial for inquiring about the truth of a given topic. As I showed, part of the aporetic tradition uses suspension in this way (Section 1.3.2). In this section, however, I will discuss another way in which suspension of belief may be used as part of a method of inquiry. That is to avail of a sort of 'pretend' and temporal suspension to assess the consequences of an argument or a hypothetical scenario. This suspension of belief is not an involuntary stance or the normative conclusion derived from a balance of evidence. You are not required to suspend your beliefs, but you are invited and allowed to do

---

[116] Transl. Rowe in Cooper & Hutchinson (1997).

it (i.e., it is epistemically permissible). The reason for suspension is the hope that it might help us find insight or the truth about a topic.

Consider, for instance, thought experiments. When we use them, we may suspend temporarily and deliberately one or more of our beliefs. When I ponder the consequences of owning a ring that can make people invisible, I suspend my belief that such a magical ring is impossible.[117] These exercises depend on our capacity to assess counterfactual scenarios as factual and take fictional narratives as schemes with real implications. We pretend not to hold some beliefs to see where that can lead us. Similarly, when we argue and ask someone to assume a hypothesis, we require them to put their beliefs into 'brackets' for the sake of the argument.[118] In these cases, suspension arises from our willingness to consider a hypothetical scenario rationally permitted under certain circumstances and rules and with specific goals in sight.[119]

Rene Descartes' (1596–1650 CE) hyperbolic doubt is perhaps the most famous and explicit example of this type of methodological suspension. It consists of intentionally withholding assent to all beliefs in things that are not absolutely certain.[120] This suspension is only an intellectual exercise, a steppingstone to finding a foundation for all knowledge. And it is only temporary and 'pretend'. One can follow the method without genuinely doubting one's beliefs, and Descartes never assumes he has offered sufficient reasons to withhold his beliefs. Descartes was well acquainted with ancient and modern revivals of scepticism, and his *Meditations* respond to the challenge they represent.[121] The question here, however, is whether ancient philosophers used suspension of belief in a similar way.

Although most ancient philosophers did not explicitly refer to suspension of belief when discussing hypothetical reasoning, they certainly assume that imagination and thought allows us to suspend our beliefs to follow these types of argumentations. Moreover, many of the arguments Descartes uses in his *Meditations* have clear antecedents in ancient philosophy. So, from

---

[117] For the original invisibility ring, see Pl. *Resp.* 2, 359a–360d.

[118] I borrow the expression from Edmund Husserl (1859–1938 CE), who appropriates the term *epochē* to mean bracketing beliefs for methodological purposes. See Husserl (1913).

[119] In other disciplines, scholars use 'suspension of disbelief'. Böcking (2008) defines it as 'an audience's tolerance of the fictionality of media content'. It involves suspending beliefs that the fictional story is believable or logical for the sake of enjoyment. Methodological suspension, as I use it here, refers to the willingness to suspend beliefs, or to entertain their suspension, for the sake of argument and discovering truth. A different case is taking a claim as a working but unendorsed hypothesis for practical purposes (see Section 3.2.2).

[120] See Descartes CSM 2:12=Cottingham, Stoothoff & Murdock (1988, vol. 2, 12); AT 7:18=Adam & Tannery (1983, vol. 7, 18); Kenny: Cottingham, Stoothoff, Murdock & Kenny (1988).

[121] See Descartes, *Meditations on First Philosophy* 1-3, Popkin (1960, chap. 9) and Forsman (2018).

a retrospective point of view, we might say that ancient philosophers used reasoning that implies this pretend methodological suspension, even if they do not conceive it in exactly that way. In what follows, I offer some examples of ancient approaches to hypothetical reasoning.

First, we have examples of what we call thought experiments.[122] Many imply a methodological suspension of belief in so far as they set up a hypothetical scenario.[123] Consider the following fragments from Xenophanes' poetry:

> ... mortals think that gods are born
> And have clothing, voice, and bodily frame just like theirs[124]
> [...]
> But if oxen, <horses> or lions had hands
> Or could draw with their hands and create works like men,
> Then horses would draw the shapes of gods like horses, and oxen like oxen,
> And they would make the same kinds of bodies
> As each one possessed its own bodily frame.[125]

Xenophanes' thought experiment requires us to suspend our beliefs about the actual abilities of oxen, horses, and lions. We must put those beliefs into 'brackets' to imagine the animals drawing their gods. Even though Xenophanes does not explicitly require us to suspend our beliefs, the analogy would not work if one completely refused to entertain the counterfactual scenario and relate it back to the real world. If someone replied to Xenophanes, 'What does it matter? These animals cannot draw!' we would rightly think the person missed the fragments' point.

We could say the same of other ancient thought experiments. For example, the Pythagorean Archytas of Tarentum (first half of the 4th century BCE) invites us to consider what would happen to someone who, standing at the outermost edge of the universe, extends his hand or his staff. One must disregard any beliefs concerning the practical impossibility of reaching this place to follow the argument.[126] Similarly, when Academic sceptics invite us to imagine what would happen if god presented us with false impressions indistinguishable

---

[122] I agree with Ierodiakonou (2018, 31) when she writes: 'There is no ancient Greek term corresponding to what we nowadays refer to as a thought experiment [...] But there is no doubt that they did use thought experiments. In fact, they often employed them in ways similar to those of contemporary philosophers, that is, both for defending their own theories as well as for refuting the theories of their opponents.' She points out that ancient Greeks refer to some of these thought experiments as *paradeigmata* (examples) or *hypodeigmata* (illustrations) and refers to Plut. *Vit. Thes.* 23.1 and Sext. Emp. *Math.* 9.431, 10.55, 10.101, 10.156, 10.347. See also Ierodiakonou (2005).

[123] But not all thought experiments require a hypothetical scenario. In cases like Theseus' ship (Plut. *Vit. Thes.* 23.1) or Carneades' plank (Cic. *Off.* 3.89-90; *Rep.* 3.30; Lactant. *Div. inst.* 5.16.10), the philosophical puzzle arises even if we refer only to factual cases.

[124] Clem. Al. *Strom.* 5.109.1=DK21B14. All transl. Laks & Most (2016).

[125] Clem. Al. *Strom.* 5.110=DK21B15.

[126] See Simpl. *in Phys.* 476.26-36. Discussed in Ierodiakonou (2011).

from true ones, one cannot complain that god would never do that. The hypothetical scenario consists of putting into brackets our beliefs about god and imagining what would happen if he behaved this way.[127]

This methodological suspension seems presupposed in other forms of hypothetical reasoning, even if we do not see them as thought experiments.[128] Take, for example, the passage in Plato's *Republic* 5, when Socrates is compelled to argue that the sharing of women and children is possible and beneficial:

> [Glaucon] '... *both* proposals could very well be disputed' [...] 'So you will have to give an argument for both.'
> [Socrates] 'I must pay the penalty. But do me this favour: let me take a holiday and act like those lazy people who make a banquet for themselves of their own thoughts when they are walking alone. People like that, as you know, do not bother to find out how any of their appetites might actually be fulfilled, so as to avoid the trouble of deliberating about what is possible and what is not. They assume that what they want is available, and then proceed to arrange all the rest, taking pleasure in going through everything they will do when they get it – thus making their already lazy souls even lazier. Well, I, too, am succumbing to this weakness at the moment and want to postpone consideration of the viability of our proposals until later. I will assume now that they are viable, if you will permit me to do so, and examine how the rulers will arrange them when they come to pass. And I will try to show that, if they were put into practice, they would be the most beneficial arrangements of all, both for the city and for its guardians. These are the things I will try to examine with you first, leaving the others for later – if indeed you will permit this.'
> 'You have my permission', Glaucon said, 'so proceed with the examination'. (*Resp.* 457e1, e7–458b8)[129]

Socrates must persuade Glaucon and his friends of two theses. The natural order would be to prove the possibility of sharing women and children first and argue for its benefit to society later. But, maybe for rhetorical reasons, Socrates wants to argue for them in reverse order.[130] For that, his interlocutors must be willing temporarily to put into parentheses their current beliefs about the possibility of sharing women and children. Notice that accepting an assumption does not necessarily involve entertaining a counterfactual scenario. We might assume what turns out to be a fact, but we take it as an assumption because we lack

---

[127] Cic. *Acad.* 2.49, Plut. *De stoic. rep.* 1057A. Compare with Descartes' deceiver god and evil demon arguments in *Meditations on First Philosophy* 1–3. For other relevant thought experiments, see Rescher (1991), Ierodiakonou (2005), Becker (2018), and Corcilius (2018).

[128] Unless, like Rescher (1991), we identify thought experimentation with any hypothetical scenario.

[129] Transl. Reeve (2004), modified.

[130] He again puts off the discussion over the sharing of women and children at 466d and addresses it once he is forced to do it at 471c–e.

sufficient evidence or proof. We suspend our actual beliefs about the matter in question to see where the argument leads.

Moreover, when we accept an assumption, we must for the sake of argument be willing to suspend other beliefs incompatible with it. If we assume that learning the history of philosophy is not a waste of time, and I tell you I spent an evening reading Plato, you cannot reply that I have wasted my time.[131] You must suspend your belief for the sake of argument.

Similarly, when we investigate a question and posit a hypothesis, the status of our hypothesis implies that we have not made up our minds about it. This means that, at least in some cases, our default position during the investigation is a genuine suspension of belief. But other times, we might believe the hypothesis is correct even if we lack definitive reasons to accept it. Instead of discarding it, we treat it as if it were true, entertaining a methodological suspension of incompatible beliefs (for hypotheses as criterion for action, see Section 4.1).

Consider the passage in Plato's *Meno* where Socrates clarifies what he means by 'hypothesis'. With regard to virtue, he confesses that 'since we don't know (*ouk ismen*) either what it is or what sort of thing it is, let us first make a hypothesis about it' (*Meno* 87b3-4). This acknowledgement of ignorance is not absolute nor prevents them from having opinions about the matter. Socrates believes that virtue relates to the soul and rapidly agrees with Meno on a series of claims that they think are obvious. Then they decide to hypothesise that virtue is a sort of knowledge (87c), and from there, they deduce that *if* that were true, it follows that virtue is teachable (89c). But Socrates later reveals some reasons to doubt this hypothesis is true. And if those reasons hold up, it will turn out that virtue is not something one can teach (89d–90c). So, we could say that Socrates' willingness to examine both hypotheses required him to bracket some of his beliefs.[132]

2.2 Irrational, Non-Rational, and Involuntary Suspension

We suspend belief irrationally when we do it voluntarily but without a balance of evidence or a permissible frame for engaging with fiction or hypothetical reasoning. However, there are various cases covered by this general claim. So let me first discuss three possible options.

(a) *Rashness*. Sometimes we suspend belief because emotions or biases make us act hastily or thoughtlessly. Consider many people's first reaction when encountering a serious accusation against a friend or family member. Even

---

[131] Unless you disagree with me on other grounds (e.g., if you do not think Plato is part of the history of philosophy).

[132] For hypothetical methods in Plato see also *Ph.* 100a-101d, and *Resp.* 6. I discuss the latter in Section 3.3.

when the charge is credible and backed up with solid evidence, people will be too quick to rally behind their loved ones, and if that is impossible, they will at least take a neutral stance, setting a higher threshold for belief formation than we would typically require.

(b) *Failures of comprehension.* If we make a mistake in weighing evidence or assessing arguments, we may suspend our beliefs when we should not. For example, when people present evidence for and against climate change to a layperson, they might think it is reasonable to suspend their belief because they do not understand the logic or recognise that one side is misrepresenting crucial information.

(c) *Disregarding evidence.* One might also suspend beliefs irrationally by purposely disregarding the evidence or force of the arguments. I could have non-epistemic reasons to prefer a neutral stance on specific topics. I might benefit from not taking sides, prefer avoiding confrontation, or withhold neutrality as a general policy in certain subjects, regardless of the evidence.

Do ancient philosophers discuss irrational suspension in these ways? I could not think of any examples of irrational suspension derived from rashness (a). It is usually the other way around. Philosophers often criticise others for their rashness in forming beliefs[133] but not for suspending them. Critics may complain about many shortcomings of the sceptics' tactics but not about how fast they jumped at suspension of belief. The reason is that suspension, as we have seen, often presupposes one has listened to both sides of an argument, studied in rival philosophical schools, or considered a plethora of empirical cases.

However, some ancient replies to scepticism contend that their arguments are fatally flawed, which we could understand as a debate about the rationality of the sceptic suspension. If the critics are right, sceptics suspend their beliefs when they should not, and thus their suspension is irrational in the second sense (b), namely as the result of faulty logic or misunderstanding of the evidence. This is often the reproach made against the sceptical Academy. For example, Cicero's character Lucullus[134] puts it as follows: 'if these Academic views are true, reason – the light and illumination of life, as we call it – is entirely done away with' (*Acad.* 2.26).[135] Later, Lucullus continues:

---

[133] See Sext. Emp. *PH* 1.20, 1.177, 1.186, 1.205, 1.212, 2.21, 3.2, 3.235, 3.280-281, *Math.* 7.155-157, and Cic. *Acad.* 2.66-68, 78.

[134] In Cicero's *Academica*, Lucullus represents the views of Antiochus of Ascalon (d. 68/9 BCE), a member of the Academy who became a dogmatist and defended a Stoic epistemology.

[135] See also *Acad.* 2.34.

> Their worst mistake, however, is to take these two radically inconsistent premises to be consistent: first, there are some false impressions (and in accepting this they own that some are true); and then again, there is no difference at all between true and false impressions. But you assumed the first premise as if there were a difference – hence the former is undermined by the latter, and the latter by the former. (*Acad.* 2.44)[136]

Some critics consider the sceptics' mistakes too obvious and evident to be honest or worth taking seriously. Take Galen (129–c.210–5 CE), who refers to the Pyrrhonian *aporia* as 'an interminable piece of nonsense' (*Temp.* 2.589).[137] This is a common reaction to radical scepticism and any view that goes against one's fundamental assumptions. From where we stand, it is sometimes hard to imagine someone questioning what we take as manifest, well established, or common knowledge. But when we are confronted with such a situation, some might think that a more charitable alternative to thinking that it is just a silly mistake is to ascribe clever dishonesty. In other passages, Galen accuses the sceptics of insincerity and subverting people, which seems to imply purposely disregarding the arguments and evidence (in one's own assessment or in its presentation to others), that is, irrationality in the third sense (c).[138]

Now consider what I call non-rational suspension. In this sense, suspension arises as a psychological reaction that happens involuntarily. A response that does not depend on any normative commitment or rational rule. In other words, this is to conceive suspension as a posture, which is affective and involuntary (like liking, disliking, and indifference), rather than as a stance we advocate or reject voluntarily. As mentioned earlier (Section 1.2), Sextus Empiricus conceives *epochē* as the affective and involuntary psychological reaction to equipollence. He describes it as a feeling (*pathos*),[139] an incapacity to decide, assert or deny, or a standstill of the intellect (*stasis dianoias*; *PH* 1.10, 26, 192–93, 195). And he considers feelings passive (hence *pathos*, from *pashein*) and unwilled, forced upon us by appearances, and not an object of investigation (*PH* 1.13, 22, 29). In the context of rational suspension, a balance of evidence offers reasons to conclude we ought to suspend judgement, but for Sextus, no decision is involved. Equipollence forces *epochē* into the sceptic. Sextus might memorise arguments, train his dialectical skills and his ability to set oppositions. But the psychological reaction is not always guaranteed; he has no control over it.

---

[136] See also *Acad.* 2.11-62, and Gal. *Aff. Pecc. Dig.* 2, 60 (Kühn)= 42 (De Boer).

[137] Transl. Singer (1997).

[138] Gal. *Dig. puls.* 8, 782-6 (Kühn), and *Opt. doc.* 1, 40-52. I come back to insincerity in Section 4.2.

[139] Sext. Emp. *PH* 1.7, 1.192, 197, 200-201, and 203. At *PH* 1.198, he calls it an 'intellectual feeling' (*pathos dianoias*).

3 What Could the Scope of Suspension Be?

Some ancient arguments and sceptical strategies raise philosophical questions about how far we can go about suspending our beliefs. For example, can we suspend all or only some of them? Is suspension restricted to a specific type of belief? Are there particular beliefs that we cannot suspend? Can someone suspend all their beliefs simultaneously, or must it be done one at a time? These questions relate to whether suspension of belief has a specific domain, and if so, why. This goes hand in hand with complex interpretative issues. For example, scholars disagree on how to read Pyrrho, Sextus Empiricus, and the Academic philosophers in this regard. Ancient sources often preserve conflicting accounts and underdetermined descriptions. Moreover, we might wonder whether some of these philosophers were implicitly committed to normative principles of rationality or implicit assumptions that clash with their self-descriptions.

In this section, I offer a sketch of how we could better distinguish the different positions at stake and then provide a brief account of the main interpretative difficulties concerning the leading representatives in Academic and Pyrrhonian scepticism. I close with a discussion on how Plato and Aristotle think about unhypothetical starting points and the scope of inquiry and *aporia*.

3.1 Ways of Restricting the Scope of Suspension

When discussing the scope of suspension of belief, the traditional taxonomy distinguishes between partial and global suspension – in other words, suspending only some or all our beliefs. 'Partial suspension' could be taken in at least two different ways. In the context of scepticism, philosophers usually take it to mean a suspension over a whole domain of beliefs, for example, all theoretical and philosophical beliefs (often labelled 'urbane' scepticism), all beliefs based on sense perception, or all moral or religious beliefs. But you do not need to be a sceptic about a whole subject. Someone who suspends some of their beliefs in different subjects would also be a partial sceptic. Moreover, some sceptical devices are topic-neutral but do not lead to a global suspension. For example, the device might apply to any belief, but one by one, being unable to guarantee suspension of all our beliefs.

'Global suspension' (sometimes 'rustic' scepticism)[140] could also mean different things because there are various ways to read the scope of the 'all' in 'I suspend all beliefs' and similar phrases. Without any qualification, it would

---

[140] The labels 'urbane' and 'rustic' used to describe types of ancient scepticism go back to Gal. *diff. puls.* 7.711K; *praenot.* 14.628K but were popularised by Barnes (1982). See also Burnyeat (1984) and Fine (1996).

mean suspending all possible beliefs, including those related to theories or circumstances one could not have imagined or considered directly. The context, however, often qualifies the scope of the sceptic's claim. For example, it could just mean all beliefs in the person's conscious mind without dismissing the possibility of forming future beliefs. Alternatively, the sceptic may have an idiosyncratic notion of belief that is narrower than others. For instance, if the sceptic defines belief as something intrinsically unclear, anything self-evident would be left outside the scope of their suspension, even if others label self-evident things as beliefs.

Scholars sometimes also use the term *radical* scepticism. But this is not the same as global suspension. As mentioned, the latter refers to the universality of the suspension. Radical scepticism instead refers to a type of scepticism and sceptical devices unrestricted in their scope and thus able to challenge the foundations of knowledge and belief justification. But notice that although global suspension presupposes radical scepticism, the reverse does not hold. It is perfectly possible, for example, that the sceptic can only evaluate one belief at a time without being able to generalise the results, even if their scepticism expands progressively. It is also possible that a strategy allows suspending any belief one wants to consider, but not all beliefs at once.

These different ways of understanding partial and global scepticism leave us with a problem. How could we establish the scope of suspension more clearly? There are at least three ways it could be restricted. One is based on the type of mental content the suspension can be about. As we have seen, suspension could leave out certain types of beliefs or other mental content by not recognising their status as beliefs, or as the sort of beliefs that suspension targets (for example, if the suspension is only directed at beliefs arrived at in a certain way). I shall call this 'type restriction'.

Another way to restrict the scope concerns whether one must be directly and currently considering the belief in question or can say to suspend beliefs indirectly; for instance, because a direct suspension implies them. I will refer to this restriction as 'direct only suspension'.

Finally, certain arguments and sceptical devices lead us only to suspend one particular and concrete belief at a time. In contrast, others invite us to suspend entire types of beliefs at once. When I am in *aporia*, I suspend one belief about a philosophical question, but that is all. I might use all my other beliefs to dig myself out of the *aporia*. But if you consider, for example, Pyrrho's argument that we should live life without beliefs, it aims at all our beliefs about the world at once (see Section. 1.3.3). So, I will refer to this as 'particular' and 'simultaneous' suspension, respectively.

Notice that these three types of restrictions do not collapse into each other. Type restriction means I suspend judgements about, for example, only religious matters, perception, or philosophical beliefs. But it says nothing about whether I suspend only beliefs I am currently considering or if I can suspend them indirectly as well. Neither does it necessarily commit me to suspend all my religious, perceptual, or philosophical beliefs at once. I might just suspend some of my beliefs, but all of them are of a specific type.[141]

No ancient philosopher attempts to suspend everything, everywhere, all at once; at least not if we mean all types of mental content without exception, simultaneously, and regardless of whether the content is considered directly or not. But, as we will see, when some ancient sceptics talk about universal *epochē*, they mean something more modest, even if this raises some concerns regarding coherence. Similarly, when we discuss partial suspension in sceptics and non-sceptics alike, it is important to notice how they restrict the scope of suspension, either because they think there are some topics or specific beliefs beyond suspension or because they delimit the inquiry in some other way.

3.2 The Scope of Academic and Pyrrhonian Scepticism

3.2.1 Arcesilaus

The scope of Arcesilaus' suspension of belief is difficult to establish. He left no writing. His philosophical method involved engaging in Socratic cross-examination and arguing for both sides of a question without revealing his views.[142] This suggests we cannot ascribe him any claim preserved in his arguments, and at the same time, we cannot rule out that he might have had some views he revealed to close associates (Sext. Emp. *PH* 1.234; cf. Cic. *Acad.* 2.60).

However, almost all sources report not only that he did not reveal his views but that he suspended all judgements. Sextus Empiricus, for example, writes that Arcesilaus 'is not found making assertions about the reality or unreality of anything, nor does he prefer one thing to another in point of convincingness or lack of convincingness, but he suspends judgement about everything' (*PH* 1.232).[143] This description puts Arcesilaus close to Pyrrhonian scepticism. However, Sextus quickly adds that, unlike the Pyrrhonists, Arcesilaus held that *epochē* was good and assent bad and that some sources say, 'he appeared to be a Pyrrhonist but in truth was a Dogmatist' (*PH* 1.233–234).

Other reports ascribe him an even stronger commitment to universal *epochē* and other doctrines (again, it is difficult to say if these are reports of his views or

---

[141] See Vázquez (2021, 99).

[142] DL 4.28, 33, 37; Euseb. *Praep. evang.* 14.7.15 (=Numen. fr. 26.107-10, Des Places); Sext. Emp. *PH* 1.234; Cic. *Acad.* 1.44-46, *Acad.* 60, *De or.* 3.67-8, 80 and 103, *Fin.* 2.1-4, *Nat. D.* 1.11, *Tusc.* 2.9.

[143] See also DL 4.33.

assessments that depend on further inferences).[144] Cicero, for instance, reports one of his arguments against Zeno as follows:

> [1] If the sage ever assents to anything, he will sometimes hold an opinion;[145]
> [2] but he will never hold an opinion;
> [3] so he won't ever assent to anything.
>
> Arcesilaus approved this argument since he supported the first and second premises. (*Acad.* 2.67)[146]

Here Arcesilaus' *epochē* is not the residual state derived from relentless philosophical cross-examination but the conclusion of an argument he is said to have accepted. However, notice that this reasoning does not commit him to *epochē* unless he also considered himself a sage, which seems unlikely since the notion of sagehood operating here is distinctively Stoic.

Cicero offers a different account in *Acad.* 1.44–5. In this passage, Arcesilaus' *epochē* derives from inapprehensibility *(akatalēpsia)*, the doctrine that nothing can be discerned or understood, and not from an argument with Stoic premises.[147] We can reconstruct it as follows:

> [1] Our senses are limited, our minds weak, and our life brief.[148]
> [2] Everything is hidden in darkness because everything is subject to opinion and custom to the point that there is no room for truth.[149]
> Given [1] and [2], then
> [3] 'nothing could be discerned or understood'.   (inapprehensibility)
> Given [3], then
> [4] 'we shouldn't assert or affirm anything or approve it with assent: we should always curb our rashness and restrain ourselves from any slip'.   (*epochē*)

Instead of a refutation of someone else's doctrines, this seems to be an argument for scepticism. The first premise is the least controversial. Most people would agree on our sensory and cognitive limitations and the brevity of human life. But the second premise makes a bold claim. Although it is difficult to deny that, in principle, everything is up for debate, why would that mean everything is hidden in darkness? The claim assumes a balance of evidence on every question. Otherwise, one could reply that not everybody's

---

[144] See Section 1.3.1 and 1.3.4. See also Cic. *Acad.* 2.77.

[145] This premise, in turn, depends on the conclusion that there are no cognitive impressions.

[146] Cf. Cic. *Acad.* 2.78.   [147] See also Cic. *Acad.* 2.59.

[148] Cf. Protagoras' reasons for his religious agnosticism (Euseb. *Prep. evang.* 14.3.7; DL 9.51=DK80B4, quoted in Section 2.1.1).

[149] This paraphrases Democritus' saying, 'in reality we know nothing for the truth is in the abyss'. DL 9.72=68DK117, transl. Graham (2010). Cf. Cic. *Acad.* 2.32, 73. For Democritus see Section 2.1.1.

opinion is worth the same. Maybe the premise depended on witnessing Arcesilaus demolish everybody else's position and argue both sides of every question.[150] If so, the aforementioned would be regarded as Arcesilaus' closing argument, which concludes with the normative recommendation that one should suspend all judgements.

The different accounts raise two questions. First, to what extent was Arcesilaus committed to universal *epochē*? And second, what would the scope of such suspension be? If Arcesilaus assented to universal *epochē*, his scepticism would be self-defeating or paradoxical (he would form the belief that he should not form any belief). Although this result would be welcome by Pyrrhonian sceptics like Sextus, most scholars offer competing interpretations to avoid such a conclusion for Arcesilaus.[151]

Some defend a 'dialectical reading' and argue that Arcesilaus was never committed to universal *epochē*. His views, if any, remain undisclosed. This is an attractive solution but, unfortunately, runs against almost all sources that explicitly attribute universal *epochē* to Arcesilaus.

Others argue that *epochē* is restricted to rational belief, which leaves weaker forms of commitment open to Arcesilaus. We can identify at least three options:

- **Psychological reactions** (i.e., postures, impulses, and desires): involuntary non-rational non-beliefs that are not normative stipulations and can be expressed as commitments that neither are beliefs nor are based on reasons.
- **Rational hypothesis:** voluntarily rational stances that fall short of belief (i.e., rational non-beliefs) and can be expressed as commitments that are not beliefs but are based on reasons.
- **Residual beliefs:** voluntary non-rational commitments which are beliefs that are not based on reasons.[152]

The first option sees Arcesilaus' commitment to *epochē* as an involuntary feeling or impulse. The second understands it as a rationally grounded supposition that falls short of belief. Finally, the last sees *epochē* as a residual belief from Arcesilaus' philosophical method, rationally unwarranted but somehow unavoidable. These three options, however, imply attributing to Arcesilaus a 'type restriction' to his suspension of belief: rational beliefs. But rational belief here means mental content we can assent to or reject consciously, which suggests that, under these interpretations, Arcesilaus'

---

[150] In doing this, Arcesilaus would also refer to the history of philosophy (Cic. *Acad.* 2.72-76, *Acad.* 1.44-46, Plut. *Adv. Col.* 26, 1121e-1122a).

[151] On this I follow Brittain & Osorio (2021a) and Brittain (2006).

[152] I build upon the distinctions in Brittain & Osorio (2021a).

epochē requires us to consider the belief in question directly, and leaves unclear whether it prohibits indirect suspension or not.

3.2.2 Carneades

Carneades' exact position concerning the scope of *epochē* is also contested.[153] His erudition and talent as a dialectician and controversialist were even greater than Arcesilaus (DL 4.62). But unfortunately, he also wrote nothing. All we know from him comes from his student Clitomachus, whose reports were passed on by Philo of Larissa (159/8–84/3 BCE) to Cicero. But things are still more complicated. Clitomachus and Philo disagreed on how to interpret Carneades, and some later sources offer misleading amalgamations of these two interpretations.[154]

According to Clitomachus, Carneades argued for inapprehensibility and universal *epochē*, just like Arcesilaus, but introducing two types of impressions and two types of assent. However, in other passages, Clitomachus depicts Carneades more dialectically, admitting that when listening to him, he could never tell which views he adhered to (Cic. *Acad.* 2.139).[155] Since Carneades' innovations in this interpretation address the practical implications of suspension, I will discuss them in Section 4. For now, I will focus only on how Philo of Larissa interpreted Carneades.

Philo thought that, unlike Arcesilaus, Carneades accepted that it is sometimes rational to hold opinions. This meant that even the sage could err, but by taking these assents as opinions and nothing more, the sage understands that nothing is apprehensible (Cic. *Acad.* 2.59).[156] Carneades, according to this interpretation, agrees with the Stoics that assent is necessary for action but disagrees with the existence of cognitive impressions. The result is a commitment to an *epochē* with a more restricted scope than that of Arcesilaus and the Clitomachean interpretation earlier. A summary of Philo's reading, or something close to it, is preserved by Eusebius:

> Carneades [. . .] applied the same method in argument as Arcesilaus, and he also adopted the practice of arguing on each side of a question and used to upset all the arguments used by others. But in the principle of *epochē* alone he differed from him, saying that it was impossible for a man to suspend judgement upon all matters, and there was a difference between 'unclear

---

[153] After Arcesilaus, the Academy was left in charge of Lacydes of Cyrene (d. c.205 BCE), and then by his students Telecles (d. c.167/6 BCE) and Evander (died some years after Telecles), who headed the school alone after Telecles became too ill to continue. Then came Hegesias (or Hegesinus) of Pergamon (dates unknown), and after him, Carneades took over (DL 4.60, Euseb. *Prep. evang.* 14.7, Cic. *Acad.* 2.16). See also Hankinson (1995, 84–86).

[154] E.g., Numen. *apud* Euseb. *Praep. evang.* 14.7.15, and Sext. Emp. *PH* 1.226.

[155] See also Numen. *apud* Euseb. *Praep. evang.* 14.8.1-10.

[156] In connection with this interpretation of Carneades, Cicero also mentions Metrodorus of Stratonice (fl. 110 BC). See *Acad.* 2.16, 2.78. But other sources seem incompatible with this report. See Brittain (2006, p. xxviii).

(*adēlon*)' and 'inapprehensible (*akatalēpton*)', and while everything was inapprehensible, not everything was unclear. He was also familiar with Stoic arguments, and he grew famous by his eristic opposition to them, aiming not at the truth, but at what appeared plausible (*phainomenon pithanon*) to the multitude. (Euseb. *Praep. evang.* 14.7.15)[157]

The last sentence seems to merge elements from the Clitomachean reading, but the main argument seems to follow Philo's interpretation:

i. Everything is inapprehensible (as Arcesilaus has argued; see [3] earlier).
ii. But not everything is unclear.
iii. Thus, there is a difference between the inapprehensible and the unclear.
iv. Humans can only suspend judgement over an issue if and only if it is unclear.
v. Therefore, humans cannot suspend judgement over everything (against [4] earlier).[158]

Scholars typically understand inapprehensibility here as the denial that there are Stoic cognitive impressions that allow knowledge. In other words, all impressions are non-cognitive (noncataleptic).[159] If so, the argument implies that sometimes we have a clear impression of things we cannot claim to know for sure. In Philo's interpretation, there is no distinction between types of assent. Therefore, it is sometimes rational to assent (strongly) to clear yet inapprehensible impressions and form opinions. But since the sage knows the clarity or persuasiveness of the impressions does not guarantee their truth value, the assent is accompanied by the understanding that there is room for being mistaken. Although this *epochē* is more restricted than the previous versions, it still contrasts with the Stoic commitment to the infallibility of the sage.[160]

3.2.3 Aenesidemus

A contemporary of Cicero, Aenesidemus criticised Academics who made strong assertions and restricted the scope of their *epochē*. According to some sources, he defected from the Academy, and took inspiration from Pyrrho to promote his version of scepticism, which later had a huge influence, especially on Sextus Empiricus. Although we only preserve a few fragments and summaries from his works, we attribute to him the ten modes of *epochē*, the eight modes against causation, and the revival of the Pyrrhonian sceptical tradition.

---

[157] Transl. Hankinson (1995, 87), modified.   [158] Cf. Hankinson (1995, 87).
[159] See Britain (2006, xxvi) and Hankinson (1995, 87).
[160] Philo's position developed from a restricted scepticism like the one he ascribes to Carneades to a fallibilism found in his Roman books. See Brittain & Osorio (2021b). For Cicero, see Brittain (2006), and Woolf (2015, chap. 2). For the decline and aftermath of the sceptical Academy, see Lévy (2010).

The sources, however, offer incompatible pictures. On the one hand, they report that Pyrrhonists like him are aporetic, entertaining doubts about every thesis and free from all dogma, determining nothing, not even that they determine nothing or that one thesis is more convincing than unconvincing.[161] On the other hand, descriptions of his position sometimes suggest that he endorsed some type of relativism or describe him as a full-on negative dogmatist, that is, someone committed to the claim that no statement of a certain type is true or no statement of a certain type is knowledgeable.[162] This has given rise to two families of competing interpretations.

According to some, Aenesidemus' brand of scepticism and scope of *epochē* is self-cancelling, topic neutral, and universal with respect to content available to the Pyrrhonian inquiry. A revisionist interpretation proposes, in contrast, that Aenesidemus' arguments do not aim at *epochē* at all but at *aporia* and the resulting negative conclusions of the type '*x* is not by nature *F*' *and* allowing relativised claims like '*x* is *F* for *y*, at time *t*, or in circumstance *C*'.[163] This second interpretation, however, has been criticised. One of the recurring objections is that the evidence does not force it and instead is incompatible with Aenesidemus' attitude towards the Academics. Moreover, it risks rendering Aenesidemus' scepticism incoherent.[164]

3.2.4 Agrippa's Five Modes

Agrippa's five modes – the mode of disagreement, regress, relativity, hypothesis, and reciprocity – are among the most powerful resources in the Pyrrhonian sceptical toolbox. Sextus Empiricus uses them extensively but simply attributes them to 'recent sceptics' (*PH* 1.164). However, Diogenes Laertius (9.89) attributes them to an Agrippa (fl. first cent. CE?) from which we know nothing else.

Like those attributed to Aenesidemus, these modes are argumentative devices used by the Pyrrhonian sceptic to guide dogmatic people towards *epochē*.[165] Modern philosophers still debate the merits of the radical epistemological challenge raised by a subset of these modes – the mode of regress, hypothesis, and reciprocity – known in the literature as Agrippa's trilemma.[166] So, it is natural to wonder about the scope of *epochē* that these modes promise to produce. However, things are not so simple.

---

[161] This claim suggests an *epochē* without any 'type restriction', but that depends on how we understand 'dogma'. On *aporia,* see Section 1.3.2, and on determining nothing, see Section 1.2.

[162] See Hankinson (1995, 288, n. 6), and Phot. *Bibl.* 212, 169b36–170a28.

[163] See Woodruff (1988) and Bett (2000, 189–222).

[164] See, e.g., Hankinson (2010, 1995, 110–16), Thorsrud (2009, 192–122), and Castagnoli (2013).

[165] Including, I take it, proto-sceptics, partial sceptics, and sceptics who relapse into dogmatism.

[166] See, e.g., Fogelin (1994), Williams (1996, 60–68), Pritchard (2000), Greco (2006, 9), Turri (2012), and Kern (2017, 39–53).

We preserve two descriptions of these modes. One in Diogenes Laertius (9.88–89) and the other in Sextus Empiricus (*PH* 1.164–169). However, there are some significant differences between these reports. The one found in Diogenes Laertius does not mention *epochē*, gives no indication that the modes can be used together, and describes them as arguments for negative dogmatism.[167] In contrast, the version presented by Sextus is explicitly dialectical, aims at *epochē*, and offers some indication of how the modes might work together. For this reason, here I will only refer to this latter version. Sextus' text reads as follows:

> According to the mode deriving from disagreement, we find that undecided (*anepikritos*)[168] dissension about the matter proposed has come about both in ordinary life and among philosophers. Because, of this we are not able either to choose or to rule out anything, and we end up with suspension of judgement. In the mode deriving from infinite regress, we say that what is brought forward as a source of conviction for the matter proposed itself needs another such source, which itself needs another, and so *ad infinitum*, so that we have no point from which to begin to establish anything, and suspension of judgement follows. In the mode deriving from relativity, as we said above,[169] the existing object appears to be such-and-such relative to the subject judging and to the things observed together with it, but we suspend judgement on what it is like in its nature. We have the mode from hypothesis when the Dogmatists, being thrown back *ad infinitum*, begin from something which they do not establish but claim to assume simply and without proof in virtue of a concession. The reciprocal mode occurs when what ought to be confirmatory of the object under investigation needs to be made convincing by the object under investigation; then, being unable to take either to establish the other, we suspend judgement about both. (*PH* 1.165–169)[170]

Sextus adds that every object of investigation can be referred to the five modes (*PH* 1.169). In other words, the sceptic can contrapose these modes to any dogmatic assertion.[171] Note, for instance, that the mode of disagreement, which Sextus always puts first,[172] applies to both philosophical and everyday

---

[167] For the discussion see Janáček (1970), Barnes (1992), and Vázquez (2019, 60–72).

[168] For the translation of *anepikritos*, see Barnes (1990, 16–20), Machuca (2011), and Vázquez (2019, 65).

[169] Reference to Sext. Emp. *PH* 1.135-6.

[170] Sextus uses the modes in multiple places, both together and separately. See *PH* 1, 170-177, 178-179, 185-186; 2, 18-20.

[171] Even if we consider self-referential assertions like 'The five modes cannot evaluate this judgement' or 'This claim cannot be the object of *epochē*'. The Pyrrhonian sceptic would simply say there is disagreement over that and then deploy the other four modes. See Vázquez (2021, 103–104).

[172] See Vázquez (2019, 72).

matters. The reach of the mode of relativity is also extremely broad; it includes anything that appears to us as a possible object of judgement. Finally, the other three modes target different attempts at justifying one's beliefs or claims to knowledge.

Given the meagre indications on how the Pyrrhonian sceptic is supposed to use them, scholars have offered different reconstructions, sometimes leaving aside the mode of relativity, disagreement or both.[173] But one way to understand their structure and use is to conceive them as a list of questions or challenges the Pyrrhonian sceptics pose to their dogmatic interlocutors or themselves whenever they feel tempted to make up their minds about something. Although Sextus does not always use them all in the same passage and often applies them in different orders or with modes from other lists, some structural things remain constant (although that only illustrates Sextus' sceptical practice and has no normative value).[174] For example, all the modes can lead to other modes or to *epochē*, disagreement always comes first, and nothing prevents the sceptic from reapplying the modes over and over, even if this means going into higher orders in the conversation (v.g., a disagreement about a disagreement and so on). An illustration of how a Pyrrhonian sceptic might use the five modes looks like the following interchange:

DOGMATIST: Marmite on toast is the best breakfast.

SCEPTIC: Isn't there some disagreement over that claim?

DOGMATIST: Well, yes. But that is because people do not use the right amount of Marmite.

SCEPTIC: Isn't that an unjustified hypothesis?

DOGMATIST: I don't think so. Whenever I have taught my friends to spread the right amount, they have changed their minds.

SCEPTIC: How does that prove anything? They could be lying to avoid hurting your feelings.

DOGMATIST: My friends would never lie to me.

SCEPTIC: How do you know? Are you going to give me another justification in need of justification, and another one, and so on?

DOGMATIST: No. Marmite just tastes better than any other breakfast.

SCEPTIC: That might seem to you, but wouldn't opinions about Marmite differ in other countries?

---

[173] See, e.g., Barnes (1990, 114–115, 116–120), Fogelin (1994, 116), Hankinson (1995, 171), Williams (2004, 121–122), Thorsrud (2009, 151), Vázquez (2009), Woodruff (2010, 226), Machuca (2015), Bullock (2016), and Sienkewicz (2019). I discuss the merits of some of these reconstructions and offer my own alternative in Vázquez (2019).

[174] Sext. Emp. *PH* 1.168, 1.170-177 (cf. DL 9.88), 1.178-179, 1.185-186, 2.18-20. See Vázquez (2019).

DOGMATIST: Yes, but they are wrong.

SCEPTIC: But if you are saying that because you believe Marmite on toast is the best breakfast, wouldn't you be presupposing what you want to prove?

As this illustration shows, when used together, the scope of application of the five modes has no thematic restriction; they are topic neutral (*PH* 1.165).[175] Moreover, by bouncing from one to the other, the Pyrrhonian sceptic can loop the conversation, never allowing any justification for our beliefs.[176]

However, it is unclear whether the five modes really aim at a global or universal *epochē*. First, someone might think these modes are implicitly committed to a normative principle of rationality. However, if they are all dialectical strategies applied by following some simple recipe, there is no need for the sceptic to believe any such principle. The dogmatist would have those commitments, not the sceptic who is only asking the questions and following impressions. But surely, one might reply, the Pyrrhonian sceptics follow certain logical rules and understand when to respond with one mode rather than the other. Could not we accuse them of believing in such things? Not really. Consider that it is possible to program machines to do all sorts of actions, including following instructions in a logical order, without beliefs of any kind.[177] This includes a chatbot programmed to respond to our knowledge claims with Agrippa's modes. Moreover, the Pyrrhonian sceptics could respond by applying the mode of disagreement and then using the other four modes to our accusation.[178] Thus, it seems that using the five modes does not imply or commit the sceptic to any belief. But could they deliver universal *epochē*?

Even if anything can be an object of *epochē*, it does not follow that the sceptic can suspend all their beliefs without any residue or that they suspend them all at once. The five modes can certainly challenge any attempt to establish a foundation or framework for knowledge and belief formation. But it does not seem that their use can deliver a general conclusion or guarantee no residue (that would require some dogmatic assumptions!). Just as the sceptic can loop the conversation and filibuster our attempts at demonstration, nothing in the five modes stop us from keep trying to offer an

---

[175] The versatility of the five modes is why I remain unpersuaded by 'urbane' readings of Sextus. But for such an interpretation, see Section 4.1, Frede (1979, 1984), and Ornelas (2021).

[176] See Vázquez (2019). [177] See Vázquez (2019, 73) and Corti (2009).

[178] This is how the Pyrrhonian sceptic would reply to attempts at 'catching Sextus out' accepting beliefs, distinctions, or norms, like those offered in Harte and Lane (1999) or Perin (2010, 2015). Alternatively, we could attribute to Sextus one of the three options mentioned in interpretations of Arcesilaus (Section. 3.2.1).

acceptable justification without committing ourselves to the idea that the explanation has to go *ad infinitum* (we might suspend judgement over that), or that the fallback position must always be suspension of judgement and not, for example, belief or disbelief with the proviso that it is open to revision or that it appeals to the best explanation. Moreover, the five modes cannot target irrationally held beliefs. Nor is it useful against the Protagorean relativism that worries Plato and Aristotle, where every opinion is true for the person having it and disagreement is impossible.[179]

3.3 Plato and Aristotle

In most ancient philosophers outside the sceptical tradition, the question is not how far their suspension of belief can go. They explicitly hold some beliefs or claim to have some knowledge. In that regard, their suspension of belief is partial.[180] They acknowledge ignorance or claim to suspend some beliefs only under specific circumstances. But we might wonder if they are, at least in principle, open to suspension of belief in every topic or if they have content restrictions: if they think there are special classes of beliefs or knowledge we simply cannot or should not suspend. Consider, for example, Epicurus. He takes the existence of bodies and void as radically fundamental (Epicurus, *Ep. Hdt.* 39–40=LS5A). Or Galen, who considers that upon analysis, even Academics agree on the undeniability of perceptually evident things (*PHP* 5.777–8). I cannot cover all relevant cases in this section, so I will only mention two examples: Plato and Aristotle.

In Plato's *Republic* 6, Socrates sketches dialectic as a method based on hypotheses similar to the one found in *Phaedo* and *Meno* (Section 2.1.2). But in *Republic* 6, the method of investigation has two moments: an upward and a downward path. The first one proceeds from hypotheses taken not as starting points to prove something else but as steppingstones to reach an unhypothetical first principle of everything. These hypotheses, Socrates explains, only use Forms to reach the unhypothetical principle. Once it is grasped, the downward path consists of reversing the direction of the investigation to go back and prove the hypotheses. Later, Socrates refers to this process as the destruction of the hypotheses, that is, the destruction of their hypothetical character (*Resp.* 7.533c). It is until then that we can claim to know the answer to our questions.[181]

---

[179] This, of course, is not the only way of interpreting Protagoras. See Section 2.1.1.
[180] Except for the Stoics, as explained in Section 1.3.4.
[181] Pl. *Resp.* 6.504a4-d3, 6.510b4-9, 6.511b2-c2, 7.533c7-d1. Cf. Arist. *Top.* 101a36-b4.

Most interpreters agree that the unhypothetical *archē* is, in fact, the Good.[182] And later, in book 7, Socrates explains:

> Unless someone can distinguish in an account the form of the good from everything else, can survive all cross-examination (*elenchōn*), as if in a battle, striving to judge things not in accordance with opinion but in accordance with being, and can come through all this with his account still intact, you'll say that he doesn't know the good itself or any other good. (*Resp.* 7.534b8-c5)[183]

The account of the unhypothetical first principle must survive all attempts at refutation, be reliable and accurate ('in accordance with being').[184] But what kind of cross-examination can there be of an unhypothetical first principle? Socrates cannot appeal to a higher hypothesis or principle and sceptics would object that it is an unjustified hypothesis. Some scholars suggest that the confirmation process must be the downward path of the method, which not only destroys the hypothetical character of the hypotheses but also is meant to confirm the status of the first principle.[185] However, at this point, a sceptic would deploy the mode of reciprocity.

Aristotle, in turn, restricts the scope of suspension in at least two ways. First, by not allowing inquiry into specific questions, and second, by also recognising an unhypothetical first principle. With regard to the first point, consider the following passage from the *Topics* 1.11 (105a3-9):

> One ought not to inquire into every problem (*problēma*) or every thesis, but only those which someone might be puzzled about (*aporēsein*) who was in need of arguments, not punishment or perception. For those who puzzle about whether one must honour the gods and care for one's parents or not need punishment, while those who puzzle about whether snow is white or not need perception.[186]

Smith (1997, 83–84) explains that the examples correspond to ethics and science. For Aristotle, Smith continues, philosophical ethics presupposes a good upbringing, which depends on dispositions formed in childhood through a process of habituation involving rewards and punishments. Likewise, if someone is unclear about an empirical fact, they should be referred to the ultimate basis of knowledge: perception. So, when an ungrateful son questions whether he is responsible for his elderly mother, Aristotle would take that as

---

[182] See, e.g., Robinson (1953, 139), Baltzly (1996, 164–165), and Benson (2015, 259); However, see Bedu-Addo (1978, 124) and Bailey (2006).

[183] Transl. Grube rev. Reeve in Cooper & Hutchinson (1997), modified.

[184] Notice the similarities of these requirements with those for the Stoic cognitive impressions (Section 1.3.4).

[185] On this point, see Benson (2015, 260–261).

[186] This passage was mentioned earlier in Section 2.1.1.

evidence of a bad upbringing that can only be treated with punishment. This suggests that even though Aristotle's research interests are wide-ranging, he has no patience for those who would 'question everything'. Does that mean Aristotle bans inquiry into some subjects and, with that, the possibility of suspending belief about them?

Smith argues that Aristotle is not restricting the scope of the investigation but is concerned instead with highlighting the limits of what one may accomplish with argument. He points out that elsewhere in the *Topics*, Aristotle has no difficulty in debating all sorts of claims. And to explain the tension, he appeals to a distinction between debating just for the sake of argument and doing it 'for real', aiming at a change in behaviour or a decision for practical purposes.

Politis (2004, 76–77), in turn, highlights the importance of *aporia* in the sense of what causes puzzlement. In Aristotle's views, he argues, not every conflict of opinion or even conflict of reputable opinions (*endoxa*) gives rise to *aporia*. The scope of the inquiry is determined by puzzlement 'because we are rationally pulled in apparently opposite and conflicting directions. But this means that one must oneself find that both sides are credible' (76). If this is correct, it explains why Aristotle is unwilling to discuss whether we should take care of our parents or whether the snow is white: he finds no puzzlement about these questions. And it does not matter that a famous philosopher like Anaxagoras argued that snow is black.[187] Aristotle feels no rational pull to doubt snow is white and probably assumes that people saying otherwise are not in genuine *aporia* either. However, this does not necessarily mean he bans inquiry into the colour of snow or filial duties for all. If anyone is in genuine *aporia* about those topics, they should inquire about them. The restriction is individualised. But does he then think there are beliefs we cannot suspend?

In *Metaphysics* Γ 3, he offers an answer. When discussing which could be the most stable first principle of all things, he claims that it must be something it is impossible to be deceived about, best known, and unhypothetical (1005b11-15). But for Aristotle, this first principle is not the Good, but the Principle of Non-Contradiction (PNC), which states: 'the same thing cannot at the same time belong and also not belong to the same thing and in the same respect (and let us assume that we have also added as many other qualifications as might be needed to respond to logico-linguistic difficulties)' (1005b19-22).[188]

---

[187] Anaxagoras argued that 'snow is frozen water and water is black and snow is therefore black' (Sext. Emp. *PH* 1.33=DK 59A97). See also *PH* 2.44, and Cic. *Acad.* 2.72, 2.100.

[188] For a different formulation, see *Metaph.* Γ.3, 1005b19-22 (and *Int.* 24b9, *Top.* 2.7, 113a23), and a comparison at Γ.6, 1011b15-22. See also *Metaph.* α.2, 996b3, Γ.3, 1006a1; *An. post.* 2.2, 53b1; *Soph. el.* 180c26.

Aristotle acknowledges that some people might deny or demand a demonstration of this principle. He focuses most of his efforts on refuting those who deny the PNC by asserting that the same thing can be and not be. According to Aristotle, this group includes Anaxagoras, Democritus, Empedocles, Heraclitus, Cratylus, and Protagoras.[189] But he also explains that uneducated people might ask for a demonstration; something that cannot be done. The first principle is, by definition, the ultimate belief. No further axioms can prove it. Otherwise, those axioms would be the first principles, or the demonstration would go on forever, which is no demonstration at all. But like in the *Republic*, Aristotle thinks it is possible to offer a demonstration by cross-examination if the interlocutor would be willing to say something meaningful to himself and another person (*Metaph.* Γ.4, 1006a11-12). And if someone is unwilling to say anything, he concludes: 'it is ridiculous to look for an argument against someone who has an argument for nothing, insofar as he has none. For such a person, insofar as he is such, is like a vegetable' (*Metaph.* Γ.4, 1006a13-15).[190]

4 What Are the Practical and Moral Implications of Suspension of Belief?

I get stressed or annoyed when I cannot decide between two or more options. Big purchases, deciding where to go for dinner, or picking a school for our children could lead to dreadful indecision. We spend lots of time making up our minds to minimise the risks of a costly mistake. In most cases, we would give anything to get out of that situation as fast as possible, provided we are not deceived. Theoretical puzzlements could lead to discomfort and despair too. Are the principles of justice I endorse the right ones, or have I been advocating for misguided and harmful policies?

These situations raise two questions I shall discuss here. The first is whether we really need to make up our minds to act. In other words: does human action require belief? And if it does, how can people who suspend belief in important practical and theoretical matters live their life? The second question concerns the psychological effects of suspension. I just described it as an unpleasant and undesirable state. Some offer a methodology to get out of these situations, but for Pyrrho (Section 1.3.3) and Sextus (Sections 1.2, 2.2), the practical outcome of suspension is *ataraxia*. How could that be, and what exactly do they mean? I conclude, however, with a question often ignored about the practical implications of suspension: is it sometimes morally problematic? Some ancient

---

[189] Arist. *Metaph.* Γ.5, 1009a6-9, a15-b15 and Γ.7, 1012a24-b2.
[190] And *An. Post.* 2.19 for his account on how we apprehend the first principles.

philosophers object to suspension by calling sceptics filibusterers and corruptors of minds. Could there be some truth to these accusations? Could someone make ill use of the sceptical strategies?

4.1 Action, Inaction, and Happiness

Many philosophers thought the scope of the Academic and Pyrrhonian suspension was exceedingly wide-ranging (even if not literally universal; see Section 3). Instead of disputing the theoretical merits of *epochē*, a famous objection turns to its practical implications. This is known as the *apraxia* or inactivity argument. In a nutshell, it points out that having no beliefs seems to render action impossible. If this is correct, then no one can live a human life suspending judgement as the sceptics recommend.

Some texts construe the objection as an accusation of hypocrisy or self-contradiction: the sceptics do not really mean what they say or negate their neutrality with their own actions. In an anecdote preserved by Diogenes Laertius (7.171=LS69C), the Stoic Cleanthes (c.330BC–c.230BC) declares that even if Arcesilaus 'destroys befitting action, he holds to it by his actions at least'. And when Arcesilaus complained that he was not flattered, Cleanthes replied, 'True. My flattery is to say that you argue one thing and do something else' (DL 7.171=LS69C).[191] If I claim I have not made up my mind about which side I support on an armed conflict or a political issue, and you later find me attending demonstrations in support of one side or another, it would be reasonable to be suspicious about my neutrality.[192] Notice that this complaint does not presuppose a wide-ranging suspension. It could be raised against one single question. But it seems more damning if the suspension is widespread.

If Arcesilaus never argued in *propria persona*, he is immune to this objection because he was not endorsing any arguments. But the Stoics assumed he advocated for global *epochē*, and as we saw, some of the evidence supports this reading (Section 3.2.1). Regardless of how we interpret Arcesilaus on this point, the debate with the Stoics could be reconstructed as follows: for the Stoics, human action requires an impulse that, in turn, requires assent to a practical impression (Section 1.3.4). It occurs to me 'It is getting late; I should eat' (impression). Once I accept this (assent), I feel compelled to open the fridge (impulse). With nothing stopping me, this is what I do (action). This framework implies that if I reject the impression or suspend my assent, I get no impulse to generate action. Arcesilaus replied, however, that action

---

[191] Transl. Long & Sedley (1987), modified. Cf. Euseb. *Praep. Evang.* 14.7.13.

[192] Scholars often treat the *apraxia* objection exclusively as a case of self-contradiction. This assumes that the sceptic is sincere but fool, whereas some ancient authors assume they were clever but insincere. Both interpretations could claim to be charitable, but for different reasons.

requires no assent, but only the impression of something appropriate and the impulse, which is compatible with *epochē* (Plut. *Adv. Col.* 1122c-d=LS69A).[193]

The Stoics retort that even if not all actions require assent, distinctively rational human action does, and thus, without assent, we cannot lead a virtuous life (Sext. Emp. *Math.* 7.158=LS69B).[194] In other words, Arcesilaus' description might not imply becoming an Aristotelian vegetable (Section 3.3), but it would be indistinguishable from the behaviour of a wild animal incapable of judgement, reflection, and the pursuit of higher ends, like virtue and happiness.

In a different passage, Arcesilaus seems to defend himself by declaring that 'he will regulate choice and avoidance and actions in general by "the reasonable" (*to eulogon*), and by proceeding following this criterion he will act rightly' (*Math.* 7.158=LS69B).[195] But what does he mean by 'the reasonable'? It could be an appropriation of a Stoic concept (Section 1.3.4). Or maybe he thought all actions were merely impulsive psychological reactions that are non-rational and non-beliefs, and that rational justification of their success could only be offered after the fact.[196] Or perhaps he thought resorting to 'the reasonable' happens only in cases of conflicting impressions.[197] However, Arcesilaus could have thought that reflection and rational thought produced reasonable impressions that motivate us to act, even if they still fall short of belief and do not require a strong assent in the Stoic sense (i.e., hypotheses, which are rational non-beliefs).[198]

According to Clitomachus' interpretation, Carneades continued and made innovations to this debate.[199] To reply to the Stoics' objection that rational human life without assent is impossible, he rejected that action presupposes assent. For that he introduced two distinctions. The first is between 'persuasive' (*pithanai*)[200] and 'unclear' (*adelai*) impressions. A persuasive impression is, like all other impressions, inapprehensible in the Stoic sense, but it is 'truth-like', and can serve as a criterion for action. In contrast, an unclear impression is not only inapprehensible but also unconvincing and obscure and, thus, useless from a practical point of view (Cic. *Acad.* 2.32–33). For example, I have the persuasive impression that swimming in the Irish sea is a terrible idea. So, even if there is no cognitive impression to settle the matter, without claiming

---

[193] Cf. Cic. *Acad.* 2.37-38.   [194] Cf. Cic. *Acad.* 2.39.   [195] Transl. Long & Sedley (1987).
[196] Ioppolo (1981, 1986).   [197] Maconi (1988, 251).
[198] This view is not without problems, see Brittain & Osorio (2021).
[199] As mentioned earlier, we preserve two competing interpretations of Carneades. I discuss Clitomachus' interpretation here, but for Philo of Larissa's, see Section 3.2.2.
[200] It is also translated as 'plausible', and following Cicero's rendering into Latin as *probabile*, as 'probable'. On why the latter might be misleading, see Hankinson (1995, 101).

knowledge or a settled opinion, I can follow my impression as my criterion of action and stay out of the water.

The second distinction Carneades makes is between two types of assent. One was the Stoic strong, dogmatic, and absolute assent. The other was what Carneades called 'approval' (*adprobatio*). The latter takes a persuasive impression and, for practical purposes, takes it as if it were true but considers it, from an epistemic point of view, an unendorsed hypothesis (Cic. *Acad.* 2.100, 104, and 109).[201] To continue my example, according to this interpretation, I would not have to assent strongly to the persuasive impression that swimming in the Irish sea is a terrible idea. I would only have to approve it as my action-guiding hypothesis. And according to Clitomachus, Carneades did not assent strongly to claims of inapprehensibility and the rationality of *epochē*. He just held them as persuasive (Cic. *Acad.* 2.210).[202]

These two distinctions allow action without a commitment to the truth of the matter. This means that living a human life requires no strong assent, only a weak form of acceptance, which responds to practical necessities. It does not imply that we have made up our minds about the question and thus the practical approval falls short of belief (i.e., they are rational hypotheses that are rational non-beliefs).

Carneades' arguments regarding the criterion for action may be more sophisticated still. According to Sextus' report (*Math.* 7.166–189), Carneades offered a modulated approach to action depending on whether one is deciding a smaller matter of everyday life, investigating a greater matter, or deciding matters that contribute to happiness. For trivialities, we can simply follow persuasive impressions since they are reliable most of the time and when they are not there is no great loss incurred. But on more important matters, we must look at the whole cluster of relevant persuasive impressions, ensuring none of them turns us away as false or unpersuasive. In essential matters like happiness, we must test in detail each of the impressions in the cluster, the abilities of the person making the judgement, the context, time, disposition, and all other relevant factors. Thus, when the stakes are high, the criterion of action must be 'simultaneously convincing, unreversed, and thoroughly tested' (*Math.* 7.166).[203] But we should notice that these are ultimately subjective criteria for action and the question remains theoretically open-ended (*PH* 1.227–228).

---

[201] See Brittain (2006, xxv–xxvii).

[202] One might worry that these theses are not directly concerned with action. But Carneades might have taken the strong Stoic assent as an action. Later, Favorinus (fl. 100 CE) explicitly extends the *pithanon* to theoretical matters. See Plut. *Quaest. conv.* 734f, Glucker (1978, 284), and Hankinson (1995, 121).

[203] Transl. Hankinson (1995, 99).

The Epicurean Colotes of Lampsacus (c.320–after 268 BC) considers a similar but distinct objection to widespread suspension: that suspension leads to arbitrary action. If no option is preferable, one could choose either since both are equally good or bad. However, Colotes protests, 'how is it that someone who suspends judgement does not rush away to a mountain instead of to the bath, or stands up and walks to the door rather than the wall when he wants to go out to the marketplace?' (Plut. *Adv. Col.* 1122e=LS69A6).[204] If the sceptics were serious about suspension', we would see them doing all sorts of heedless and unconventional things at least as often as common activities. Since we do not, their behaviour casts doubt on their sincerity or consistency.

One exception comes to mind, though. In a report preserved in Diogenes Laertius (9.62=LS1A4), we read that Pyrrho took no precautions in his daily life nor avoided anything, including oncoming wagons, falling off cliffs, or facing aggressive dogs, surviving only thanks to the help of his friends who kept him safe. Many take this report as a fabricated story based on Aristotle's arguments against deniers of the Principle of Non-Contradiction (*Metaph.* Γ 1008b).[205] But Beckwith (2015, 185) suggests that both versions could derive from reports of an Indian sect by chroniclers of Alexander the Great's expedition to Gandhāra. In any case, in the same paragraph Diogenes reports a contrasting account by Aenesidemus, who said that despite embracing *epochē*, Pyrrho was not careless.

Other texts support Aenesidemus' account and insist that Pyrrho led a life of almost perfect imperturbability, tranquillity, and little regard for social conventions. But if his suspension did not entail arbitrary action, but only calm in the face of life's hardships, what was Pyrrho's criterion for action? We lack decisive evidence on this point. Bett (2000, ch. 3) thinks that despite Pyrrho's mistrust of his faculties, he still acted in accordance with what things appeared to him, only in an unopinionated and uncommitted way. However, if what Pyrrho argues is that our opinions and sensations do not tell us the truth or lie in a reliable way,[206] he could still say he follows his opinions and sensations in action, only with less confidence than a dogmatic would, not granting them the capacity to perturb his peace of mind.

Sextus Empiricus dedicates one of the first chapters of his *Outlines* (1.21–24) to discussing the sceptic's criterion for action.[207] He rejects that the sceptic

---

[204] Transl. Long & Sedley (1987).   [205] See Bett (2000, 67–69).

[206] This depends on how we read *alētheuein* in the first sentence of the Aristocles' passage (quoted in Section 1.3.3). Bett (2000, 59) argues that the sentence means that 'any given sensation, or any given opinion, is neither truth nor false'. But others like Brennan (1998, 417) understand that our sensations and opinions 'do not reliably or constantly tell the truth or lie'.

[207] See also Sext. Emp. *Math.* 11.162-166; DL 9.104-105.

would be inactive and says that 'the criterion of the sceptical lifestyle is what is apparent, implicitly meaning by this the appearances; for they depend on passive and unwilled feelings and are not objects of investigation' (1.22). There has been much discussion over how to interpret Sextus on this point and whether his criterion for action implies that he holds some beliefs or dogmas.[208]

Sextus says, for example, that the sceptics assent to the appearances (*PH* 1.19), and that this includes 'everyday observances' which include 'guidance by nature, necessitation by feelings, handing down of laws and customs, and teachings of kinds of expertise' (*PH* 1.23).[209] He even claims that in the general sense of 'belief' (*dogma*) as 'acquiescing', the sceptic does hold beliefs (*PH* 1.13). And we might even say that they are not mere beliefs but dogmas in a paradigmatic way: since they are not objects of investigation, they are not up for debate. If we challenge Sextus for following a law that we think is unjust, he could simply end the discussion by replying that it appears just to him.[210] So, in this sense, Sextus is not only a dogmatist but dogmatic: his beliefs are unquestionable and immune to criticism. Combined with the inclusion of received laws and customs in the list of appearances he follows, we might worry that Sextus' project could justify the most reactionary of attitudes. The advantage of this reading of Sextus is, obviously, that if he holds unquestionable dogmas, he does not have to worry about the *apraxia* or arbitrary action objections.

Sextus might not be as dogmatic as this 'urban' interpretation suggests (see Section 3.2.4). But even if he is a more 'rustic' sceptic, and his avowals to appearances convey an attitude different from or weaker than belief, they too are subjective and unquestionable. It is worth noticing that, unlike religious fundamentalists who hold fixed dogmas, the sceptics' appearances might change from one day to the other or from one instant to the other, unwillingly. So, we could understand Sextus' attitudes towards appearances not as stances based on beliefs but as postures, that is affective and involuntary psychological reactions that are non-rational non-beliefs. They are analogous to liking: if someone likes vanilla ice cream, that person can withhold or lie about that liking, yet have no control over it. Likewise, something appears in a certain way and not in another, and one could lie about the appearance but cannot change one's involuntary psychological reaction. And, importantly, one can act and live just by following these appearances, even if they are not beliefs or stances. Sextus, of course, does

---

[208] See Burnyeat & Frede (1997), Fine (2000), Barnes (2007), and Perin (2010).

[209] See also *PH* 1.226.

[210] Pyrrhonian sceptics are happy to oppose appearances to other appearances and arguments, but all lead to *epochē* about the facts and the nature of things. The sceptics can still act on their personal appearances.

not affirm or deny having this feeling he calls *epochē*. He only offers a descriptive report of what happens to him at a specific time and place (*PH* 1.4, 15, 197, 203).

Like the Stoics, we could object that following one's appearances does not allow for a fully rational life and the pursuit of virtue and happiness. But Sextus includes perceiving and thinking as part of 'nature's guidance' (*PH* 1.24; cf. *Math.* 8.203). Moreover, he testifies that the sceptic has found *ataraxia*. This result, we read, is fortuitous, and there is no guarantee it will work on others. If Sextus were to claim something like that, we could accuse him of proposing an obscure dogmatic theory. But Sextus never claims that the equipollence that produces *ataraxia* for him will necessarily do so for others. It might, but it might not. However, since the reward is *ataraxia*, he hopes that sharing his discovery might help some people overcome rashness. When he deploys the modes or other sceptical devices, he does not offer them as arguments to persuade via their soundness and our commitments to rational principles. On the contrary, he provides them as therapy (*PH* 1.26). Like a proper doctor, he offers no panacea to dogmatism but shares a treatment with some reported success. If I feel anxious or troubled by suspension, it might not be the right treatment for me, but it does not necessarily follow that others will not benefit.

Moreover, I could have misread the situation. Sextus recognises that indecision could disrupt our tranquillity, and we might think that deciding will bring it back. But Sextus seems to suggest that stable tranquillity derives from the widespread suspension that comes after the realisation that 'to every account an equal account is opposed' (*PH* 1.12), so no determination about which things are good or bad have any place, which allows us to stop pursuing or avoiding things with the intensity that comes from believing that things are really good or bad (*PH* 1.28; 3.168–218; *Math.* 11.1–109).

At this point, some people might feel that Sextus is cheating. He seems to be saying two incompatible things: that the sceptic keeps inquiring open and, at the same time, obtains tranquillity from realising that equipollence is pervasive. However, Sextus has some resources to reply to this criticism. He could, for example, deploy Agrippa's modes or say that realising that equipollence is pervasive is itself not a dogma but an appearance.

4.2 Filibusterers and Corruptors of Minds

Some ancient philosophers were harsh critics of widespread withholding or suspension of beliefs. I already mentioned Galen (Section 2.2). Another example is Numenius (2nd to 3rd centuries CE), who refers to Carneades as a conjurer and filibusterer, able to enslave and corrupt minds.[211] Given that this assessment invokes the accusation levelled at Socrates of corrupting the youth,[212] Carneades might have been flattered. But Numenius thought that what Carneades does is morally problematic. Numenius interprets Carneades in a dialectical way, assuming he never argued in *propria persona* but that, in private, he agreed to and affirmed things like any other person. His criticism is not that Carneades contradicts himself but that he taught opposing arguments that only confused weaker minds while he kept his own views private. In other words, Numenius considers Carneades a merchant of doubt:[213] someone who spreads doubt and confusion to keep a discussion alive, make people suspend judgement or become agnostic, when, in fact, has settled views about the topics but benefits from other people's doubt.

Numenius' assessment is most probably unfair. Carneades' method could have a pedagogical intent: to make people think for themselves. However, the criticism raises an interesting question about using and misusing sceptical strategies. For example, should we always be allowed to argue both sides of a question? The sceptics presuppose that we are, but non-sceptics disagree.

Aristotle thinks that 'a person is necessarily in a better position to make a judgment when – as if they were opposing parties in a court case – he has heard all the contending arguments' (*Metaph.* B.1, 995b1-4). But there is a condition. For Aristotle, one must be in genuine *aporia*. He has little patience for eristics and filibustering (Section 3.3). In contrast, Zeno of Citium thinks we should not listen to both sides of a debate (for or against a claim). We only need to hear the first speaker:

> The second speaker [in a debate] must not be heard, whether the first speaker proved his case (for the inquiry is then finished) or did not prove it (for that is just like his not having complied when summoned, or his having complied by talking nonsense). But either he proved his case or he did not prove it. Therefore, the second speaker must not be heard. (Plut. *De stoic. rep.* 1034E=LS31 L)[214]

However, later Stoics like Chrysippus allowed the exploration of both sides of a question if it was done carefully (Plut. *De stoic. rep.* 1036A). Crucially, like Aristotle, Chrysippus assumes the investigation is carried out conscientiously and in good faith. Plato, in contrast, considers some scenarios where interlocutors are insincere, hostile, or epistemically insouciant. But Plato's Socrates continuously tries to secure sincere answers and common ground. When that fails, the conversation often falls apart.

---

[211] See Numen. *apud* Euseb. *Praep. evang.* 14.8, and 14.6.2 for his assessment of Arcesilaus.
[212] Pl. *Euthyphr.* 2b-3b; *Ap.* 24b-c.　　　[213] I borrow the label from Oreskes & Conway (2011).
[214] Transl. Long & Sedley (1987).

The problem is that someone could avoid agreeing with us on anything and then use sceptical tactics to obstruct an investigation or stall a decision-making process. After all, someone using sceptical modes could filibuster a conversation by continually challenging the premises of any new argument.[215] Many sceptical questions and methods will be perfectly acceptable in any debate or inquiry. Even worse, people's sincerity and intentions in such a context would be difficult to assess. We might know that someone has a vested interest in not reaching an agreement or a decision, and we might be suspicious about their aims. However, if the person only asks appropriate questions and cross-examines both sides of every issue, they will look like a fair and thorough participant who simply aims to prevent rashness. And any attempts at moving forward without addressing their questions would seem unfair (which is why such tactics are effective in the first place).

Yet, there are other ethical considerations: Is spending too much time considering two sides of an issue potentially harmful, especially when most people (or specialists) agree that the prospects of equipollence are low? Is it unwise to always offer the same platform to both sides of an issue? Consider journalists who feel committed to offering everyone equal airtime, even if someone holds indefensible views or is known as a liar or deceiver. Or think of policymakers who want to include debunked conspiracy theories in the education curriculum. Or cases in which there is an urgency to our deliberations?[216] What would the best approach be? For now, I leave the question open.

---

[215] See Prakken (2005, 1019).
[216] For the tension between political expediency and the leisure to take as long as is philosophically needed, see Allen (1996).

References

Adamson, P. (2015) *Philosophy in the Hellenistic & Roman Worlds*. Oxford: Oxford University Press.

Allen, D. (1996) 'A Schedule of Boundaries: An Exploration, Launched from the Water-Clock, of Athenian Time'. *Greece & Rome*, 43(2), 157–168.

Annas, J., & Barnes, J. (1985) *The Modes of Scepticism*. Cambridge: Cambridge University Press.

Annas, J. & Barnes, J. (eds.) (2000) *Sextus Empiricus. Outlines of Scepticism*. Cambridge: Cambridge University Press.

Atkins, P. (2017) 'A Russellian Account of Suspension of Judgement', *Synthese*, 194(8), 3021–3046.

Bailey, D. T. J. (2006). 'Plato and Aristotle on The Unhypothetical', *Oxford Studies in Ancient Philosophy*, 30, 101–126.

Daltzly, D. C. (1996) '"To an Unhypothetical First Principle" in Plato's Republic', *History of Philosophy Quarterly*, 13(2), 149–165.

Barnes, J. (1979) *The Presocratic Philosophers*. New York: Routledge.

(1982) 'The Beliefs of a Pyrrhonist', *Proceedings of the Cambridge Philological Society* (28), 1–29.

(1990) *The Toils of Scepticism*. New York: Cambridge University Press.

(1992) 'Diogenes Laertius IX 61–116: The Philosophy of Pyrrhonism', in Hasse, W., & Temporini, H. (eds.) *Aufstieg und Niedergang der römischen Welt*. Berlin: de Gruyter, pp. 4241–4301.

(2007) 'Sextan Scepticism', in Scott, D. (ed.) *Maieusis*. Oxford: Oxford University Press, 322–34.

Becker, A. (2018) 'Thought Experiments in Plato', in Stuart, M. T., Fehige, Y., & Brown, J. R. (eds.) *The Routledge Companion to Thought Experiments*. London: Brill, pp. 44–56.

Beckwith, C. I. (2015) *Greek Buddha: Pyrrho's Encounter with Early Buddhism in Central Asia*. Princeton: Princeton University Press.

Bedu-Addo, J. T. (1978) 'Mathematics, Dialectic and the Good in the *Republic* VI-VII', *Platon*, 30, 111–127.

Benson, H. H. (2015) *Clitophon's Challenge: Dialectic in Plato's Meno, Phaedo, and Republic*. New York: Oxford University Press.

Bett, R. (1994) 'Aristocles on Timon on Pyrrho: The Text, Its Logic, and Its Credibility', *Oxford Studies in Ancient Philosophy*, 12, 137–181.

(2000) *Pyrrho, his Antecedents, and his Legacy*. Oxford: Oxford University Press.

(2002) 'What Does Pyrrhonism Have to Do with Pyrrho?', in Sihvola, J. (ed.) *Ancient Scepticism and the Sceptical Tradition*. Helsinki: Acta Philosophica Fennica, 11–33.

(ed.) (2005) *Sextus Empiricus: Against the Logicians*. Cambridge: Cambridge University Press.

Böcking, S. (2008) 'Suspension of Disbelief', in Donsbach, W. (ed.) *The International Encyclopedia of Communication*. Wiley & Sons. https://doi.org/10.1002/9781405186407.wbiecs121.

Bonazzi, M. (2021). *Sophists*. Cambridge: Cambridge University Press.

Brennan, T. (1996) 'Reasonable Impressions in Stoicism', *Phronesis*, 41(3), 318–334.

(1998) 'Pyrrho on the Criterion', *Ancient Philosophy*, 18, 417–434.

(2000) 'Reservation in Stoic Ethics', *Archiv fur Geschichte der Philosophie*, 82(2), 149–177.

Brittain, C. (ed.) (2006) *Cicero: On Academic Scepticism*. Indianapolis: Hackett.

Brittain, C., & Osorio, P. (2021a) 'Arcesilaus', in Zalta, E. N. (ed.) *The Stanford Encyclopedia of Philosophy*. https://plato.stanford.edu/archives/fall2021/entries/arcesilaus/.

(2021b) 'Philo of Larissa', in Zalta, E. N. (ed.) *Stanford Encyclopedia of Philosophy*. https://plato.stanford.edu/archives/sum2021/entries/philo-larissa/.

Brunschwig, J. (1994) 'Once Again on Eusebius on Aristocles on Timon on Pyrrho', in *Papers in Hellenistic Philosophy*. Cambridge: Cambridge University Press, pp. 190–211.

(1996) 'Le Fragment DK70B1 de Métrodore de Chio', in Algra, K., van der Horst, P., & Runia, D. (eds.) *Polyhistor*. Leiden: Brill, pp. 21–38.

(2017) 'Democritus and Xeniades', in Graham, D. W., & Caston, V. (eds.) *Presocratic Philosophy*. London: Routledge (first published by Ashgate in 2002), pp. 175–184.

Bullock, J. B. (2016) 'The Challenges of the Modes of Agrippa', *Apeiron*, 49(4), 409–435.

Burnyeat, M. (1980) 'Tranquility Without a Stop: Timon, Frag. 68', *Classical Quarterly*, 30, 86–93.

(1984) 'The Sceptic in his Place and Time', in Rorty, R., Schneewind, J. B., & Skinner, Q. (eds.) *Philosophy in History*. Cambridge: Cambridge University Press, pp. 225–254.

Burnyeat, M., & Frede, M. (eds.) (1997) *The Original Sceptics: A Controversy*. Indianapolis: Hackett.

Cassam, Q. (2019) *Vices of the Mind*. Oxford: Oxford University Press.

Castagnoli, L. (2000) 'Self-bracketing Pyrrhonism', *Oxford Studies in Ancient Philosophy*, 18, 263–328.

(2013) 'Early Pyrrhonism: Pyrrho to Aenesidemus', in Warren, J., & Sheffield, F. (eds.) *Routledge Companion to Ancient Philosophy*. New York: Routledge, pp. 496–510.

(2018) '*Aporia* and Enquiry in Ancient Pyrrhonism', in Karamanolis, G. E., & Politis, V. (eds.) *The Aporetic Tradition in Ancient Philosophy*. Cambridge: Cambridge University Press, pp. 205–227.

Chiesara, M. L. (2004) *Storia dello sceticismo grego*. Turin: Giulio Einaudi.

Cooper, J. M. and Hutchinson, D. S. (eds.) (1997) *Plato Complete Works*. Indianapolis: Hackett.

Corcilius, K. (2018) 'Aristotle and Thought Experiments', in Stuart, M. T., Fehige, Y., & Brown, J. R. (eds.) *The Routledge Companion to Thought Experiments*. London: Routledge, pp. 57–76.

Corti, L. (2009) *Scepticisme et Langage*. Paris: Vrin.

Cottingham, J., Stoothoff, R., Murdoch, D., & Kenny, A. (eds) (1988) *The Philosophical Writings of Descartes*, 3 vols. Cambridge: Cambridge University Press.

Couissin P. (1929) 'L'origine et révolution de l'ἐποχή', R*evue des Études Grecques*, 42(198), 373–397.

Crawford, S. (2004) 'A Solution for Russellians to a Puzzle about Belief', *Analysis*, 64(3), 223–229.

Crisp, R. (ed.) (2000) *Aristotle Nicomachean Ethics*. Cambridge: Cambridge University Press.

Curd, P. (2001) 'Why Democritus was not a Skeptic', in Preus, A. (ed.) *Before Plato: Essays in Ancient Greek Philosophy, vi*. Albany: SUNY Press, pp. 149–69.

Davis, W. (2024) 'Implicature', in Zalta, E. N. & Nodelman U. (eds.), *The Stanford Encyclopedia of Philosophy (Spring 2024 Edition), forthcoming*. https://plato.stanford.edu/archives/spr2024/entries/implicature/.

Decleva Caizzi, F. (1981) *Pirrone Testimonianze*. Napoli: Bibliopolis.

(1992) 'Aenesidemus and the Academy', *Classical Quarterly*, 42, 176–189.

DePaul, M. R. (2004) 'Truth, Consequentialism, Withholding, and Proportioning Belief to the Evidence', *Philosophical Issues*, 14(1), 91–112.

Descartes, R. (1983) *Oeuvres De Descartes, 11 vols*. Edited by C. Adam & P. Tannery. Paris: J. Vrin.

Dillon, J. M. & Blumenthal, H. J. (eds.) (2015) Plotinus. Ennead IV.3-4.29. Las Vegas: Parmenides.

Fine, G. (1996) 'Scepticism, Existence, and Belief', *Oxford Studies in Ancient Philosophy*, 14, 273–290.

(2000) 'Sceptical *Dogmata*: Outlines of Pyrrhonism I 13', *Methexis*, 12, 81–105.

Flintoff, E. (1980) 'Pyrrho and India', *Phronesis*, 25, 88–108.

Fogelin, R. J. (1994) *Pyrrhonian Reflections on Knowledge and Justification*. New York: Oxford University Press.

Forsman, J. (2018) 'Descartes and the Suspension of Judgment – Considerations of Cartesian Skepticism and *Epoché*', *Proceedings of the XXIII World Congress of Philosophy*, 70, 15–20.

van Frassen, B. C. (1998) 'The Agnostic Subtly Probabilified', *Analysis*, 58(3), 212–220.

(2004) 'Replies to Discussion on The Empirical Stance', *Philosophical Studies*, 121, 171–92.

Frede, M. (1979) 'The Skeptic's Beliefs', in Burnyeat, M. F., & Frede, M. (eds.) *The Original Sceptics*. Indianapolis: Hackett, pp. 1–24.

(1984) 'The Skeptic's Two Kinds of Assent and the Question of the Possibility of Knowledge', in Rorty, R., Schneewind, J. B., & Skinner, Q. (eds.) *Philosophy in History*. Cambridge: Cambridge University Press, pp. 255–278.

Friedman, J. (2013a) 'Question-Directed Attitudes', *Philosophical Perspectives*, 27(1), 145–174.

(2013b) 'Rational Agnosticism and Degrees of Belief', *Oxford Studies in Epistemology*, 4, 57–81.

(2013c) 'Suspended Judgment', *Philosophical Studies*, 162(2), 165–181.

(2017) 'Why Suspend Judging?', *Nous*, 51(2), 302–326.

Gagarin, M. (2002). 'Protagoras' New Fragment: Thirty Years Later', *Noctes Atticae*, 34, 114–120.

Glucker, J. (1978) 'Antiochus and the Late Academy', *Hypomnemata*, 56. Göttingen: Vandenhoeck & Ruprecht, p. 510.

Graham, D. W. (ed.) (2010) *The Texts of Early Greek Philosophy*, 2 vol. Cambridge: Cambridge University Press.

Greco, J. (2006) 'Virtue, Luck and the Pyrrhonian Problematic', *Philosophical Studies*, 130(1), 9–34.

(2017) 'Was Pyrrho a Pyrrhonian?', *Apeiron*, 50(3), 335–365.

Grgic, F. (2014) 'Investigative and Suspensive Scepticism', *European Journal of Philosophy*, 22(4), 653–673.

Groarke, L. (1990) *Greek Scepticism: Anti-Realist Trends in Ancient Thought*. Montreal: McGill- Queen's University Press.

Hájek, A. (1998) 'Agnosticism meets Bayesianism', *Analysis*, 58(3), pp. 199–206.

Hankinson, R. J. (1995) *The Sceptics*. New York: Routledge.

(2010) 'Aenesidemus and the Rebirth of Pyrrhonism', in Bett, R. (ed.) *The Cambridge Companion to Ancient Scepticism*. Cambridge: Cambridge University Press, 105–119.

Harte, V., & Lane, M. (1999) 'Pyrrhonism and Protagoreanism. Catching Sextus Out?', *Philosophiegeschichte und Logische Analyse*, 2, 157–72.

Henry, J. (2022). 'The Agnosticism of Protagoras', *Revue de philosophie ancienne*, XL, 213–243.

Husserl, E. (1913) *Ideas Pertaining to a Pure Phenomenology and to a Phenomenological Philosophy – First Book*. Edited by F. Kersten. Hague: Nijhoff (1982).

Ierodiakonou, K. (2005) 'Ancient Thought Experiments: A First Approach', *Ancient Philosophy*, 25(1), 125–140.

(2011) 'Remarks On The History Of An Ancient Thought Experiment''', in Ierodiakonou, K., & Roux, S. (eds.) *Thought Experiments in Methodological and Historical Contexts*. Leiden: Brill, pp. 37–50.

(2018) 'The Triple Life of Ancient Thought Experiments', in Stuart, M. T., Fehige, Y., & Brown, J. R. (eds.) *The Routledge Companion to Thought Experiments*. London: Routledge.

Inwood, B., & Gerson, L. P. (eds.) (2008) *The Stoics Reader: Selected Writings and Testimonia*. Indianapolis: Hackett.

Ioppolo, A. M. (1981) *Il concetto di 'eulogon' nella filosofia di Arcesilao*. Naples: Bibliopolis.

(1986) *Opinione e Scienza*. Napoli: Bibliopolis.

Jackson, E. G. (2020) 'The Relationship between Belief and Credence', *Philosophy Compass*, 15(6), 1–13.

Janáček, K. (1970) 'Skeptische Zweitropenlehre und Sextus Empiricus Eirene', *Eirene*, 8, 47–55.

Karamanolis, G., & Politis, V. (eds.) (2018) *The Aporetic Tradition in Ancient Philosophy*. Cambridge: Cambridge University Press.

Kerferd, G. B. (1981) *The Sophistic Movement*. Cambridge: Cambridge University Press.

Kern, A. (2017) *Sources of Knowledge*. Cambridge, MA: Harvard University Press.

Laks, A., & Most, G. W. (eds.) (2016) *Early Greek Philosophy. Volume III, Part 2*. Cambridge, MA: Harvard University Press.

Lammenranta, M. (2008) 'The Pyrrhonian Problematic', in Greco, J. (ed.) *The Oxford Handbook of Skepticism*. Oxford: Oxford University Press, 9–33.

Lee, M. K. (2005) *Epistemology after Protagoras*. Oxford: Clarendon Press.

Lesses, G. (2002) 'Pyrrho the Dogmatist', *Apeiron*, 35(3), 255–271.

Lévy, C. (2010) 'The Sceptical Academy: Decline and Afterlife', in Bett, R. (ed.) *The Cambridge Companion to Ancient Scepticism*. Cambridge: Cambridge University Press, pp. 81–104.

Lipton, P. (2004) 'Discussion: Epistemic Options', *Philosophical Studies*, 121(2), 147–158.

Long, A. A. (1974) *Hellenistic Philosophy*. London: Routledge.

(2006) *From Epicuris to Epictetus*. Oxford: Clarendon Press.

Long, A. A., & Sedley, D. N. (1987) *The Hellenistic Philosophers. 2 Vols.* Cambridge: Cambridge University Press.

Lord, E. (2020) 'Suspension of Judgment, Rationality's Competition, and the Reach of the Epistemic', in Schmidt, S., & Ernst, G. (eds.) *The Ethics of Belief and Beyond*. Abindon: Routledge, pp. 126–145.

Machuca, D. E. (2011) 'The Pyrrhonian Argument from Possible Disagreement', *Archiv für Geschichte der Philosophie*, 93(2), 148–161.

(2015) 'Agrippan Pyrrhonism and the Challenge of Disagreement', *Journal of Philosophical Research*, 40, 23–39.

Maconi, H. (1988) '*Nova Non Philosophandi Philosophia*: A Review of Anna Maria Ioppolo, *Opinione e Scienza*', *Oxford Studies in Ancient Philosophy* 6, 231–253.

Mansfeld, J. (1995) 'Aenesidemus and the Academics', in Ayers, L. (ed.) *The Passionate Intellect*. London: Routledge, pp. 235–248.

Mansfeld, J. (2018) *Studies in Early Greek Philosophy*. Leiden: Brill, pp. 332–352.

Masny, M. (2020) 'Friedman on Suspended Judgment', *Synthese*, 197(11), 5009–5026.

McGrath, M. (2021) 'Being Neutral: Agnosticism, Inquiry and the Suspension of Judgment', *Nous*, 55(2), 463–484.

Mensch, P. (2018) *Diogenes Laertius. Lives of Eminent Philosophers*. Edited by J. Miller. New York: Oxford University Press.

Monton, B. (1998) 'Bayesian Agnosticism and Constructive Empiricism', *Analysis*, 58(3), 207–212.

Moon, A. (2018) 'The Nature of Doubt and a New Puzzle about Belief, Doubt, and Confidence', *Synthese*, 195(4), 1827–1848.

Morel, P.-M. (1996) *Démocrite et la recherche des causes: Préface de Jacques Brunschwig*. Paris: Klincksieck.

Natali, C. (2008) 'Socrates' Dialectic in Xenophon's *Memorabilia*', in Judson, L., & Karasmanis, V. (eds.) *Remembering Socrates*. New York: Oxford University Press, pp. 3–19.

Oreskes, N., & Conway, E. M. (2011). *Merchants of Doubt*. London: Bloomsbury.

Ornelas, J. (2021) 'Sképsis escéptica: contra la interpretación rústica del pirronismo sexteano', in J. Ornelas, (ed.) *Rústicos versus Urbanos*. Mexico City: UNAM, pp. 75–88.

Palmer, J. (2018) 'Contradiction and *Aporia* in Early Greek Philosophy', in Karamanolis, G., & Politis, V. (eds.) *The Aporetic Tradition in Ancient Philosophy*. Cambridge: Cambridge University Press, pp. 9–28.

Patrick, M. M. (1929) *The Greek Sceptics*. New York: Columbia University Press.

Perin, C. (2010) *The Demands of Reason*. Oxford: Oxford University Press.

 (2015) 'Skepticism, Suspension of Judgment, and Norms for Belief', *International Journal for the Study of Skepticism*, 5(2), 107–125.

Politis, V. (2004) *Aristotle and the Metaphysics*. London: Routledge.

 (2018) '*Aporia* and Sceptical Argument in Plato's Early Dialogues', in Politis, V., & Karamanolis, G. E. (eds.) *The Aporetic Tradition in Ancient Philosophy*. Cambridge: Cambridge University Press, pp. 48–66.

Prakken, H. (2005) 'Coherence and Flexibility in Dialogue Games for Argumentation', *Journal of Logic and Computation*, 15(6), 1009–1040.

Popkin, R. (1960) *The History of Scepticism from Erasmus to Descartes*. Assen: Van Gorcum.

Powell, J. G. F. (2013) 'The Embassy of the Three Philosophers to Rome in 155 bc', in Kremmydas, C., & Tempest, K. (eds.) *Hellenistic Oratory*. Oxford: Oxford University Press. pp. 219–247.

Pritchard, D. (2000) 'Doubt Undogmatized: Pyrrhonian Scepticism, Epistemological Externalism and the "Metaepistemological" Challenge', *Principia*, 4(2), 187–214.

Raleigh, T. (2021) 'Suspending is Believing', *Synthese*, 198(3), 2449–2474.

Reeve, C. D. C. (ed.) (2004) *Plato: Republic*. Indianapolis: Hackett.

 (ed.) (2016) *Aristotle: Metaphysics*. Indianapolis: Hackett.

Rescher, N. (1991) 'Thought Experimentation in Pre-Socratic Philosophy', in Horowitz, T., & Massey, G. (eds.) *Thought Experiments in Science and Philosophy*. Savage: Rowman & Littlefield, pp. 31–41.

Robinson, R. (1953) *Plato's Earlier Dialectic*. 2nd ed. Oxford: Oxford University Press.

Roeber, B. (2019) 'Evidence, Judgment, and Belief at Will', *Mind*, 128(511), 837–859.

Russell, B. (1953) 'What is an Agnostic?', in *Look Magazine (reprinted in The Basic Writings of Bertrand Russell, London: Routledge 2009)*. London: Routledge, pp. 557–565.

Salles, R., & Boeri, M. (2014) *Los filósofos estóicos*. Sankt Augustin: Academia Verlag.

Salmon, N. (1986) *Frege's Puzzle*. Cambridge, MA: MIT Press.

 (1989) 'Illogical Belief', *Philosophical Perspectives*, 3, 243–285.

Sedley, D. N. (2002) 'The Origins of the Stoic God', in Frede, D., & Laks, A. (eds.) *Traditions of Theology*. Leiden: Brill, pp. 41–83.

Sellars, J. (2006) *Stoicism*. Durham: Acumen.

Seuss (1957) *How the Grinch Stole Christmas!* New York: Random House.

Sienkewicz, S. (2019) *Five Modes of Scepticism*. Oxford: Oxford University Press.

Singer, P. N. (ed.) (1997) *Galen: Selected Works*. Oxford: Oxford University Press.

Smith, R. (ed.) (1997) *Aristotle: Topics, Books I and VIII*. Oxford: Clarendon Press.

Snyder, C. (2018) 'On the Teaching of Ethics from Polemo to Arcesilaus', *Études platoniciennes [Online]*, 14. DOI: https://doi.org/10.4000/etudes-platoniciennes.1260

de Souza, S., & Vázquez, D. (2019) 'Teleology and Sophistic Endeavour in the *Euthydemus*', *Australasian Philosophical Review*, 3(2), 183–190.

Staffel, J. (2019) 'Credences and Suspended Judgments as Transitional Attitudes', *Nous-Supplement*, 29(1), 281–294.

Stopper, M. R. (1983) 'Schizzi Pirroniani', *Phroensis*, 28(3), 265–297.

Stough, C. L. (1969) *Greek Skepticism: A Study in Epistemology*. Berkeley: University of California Press.

Sturgeon, S. (2010) 'Confidence and Coarse-Grained Attitudes', *Oxford Studies in Epistemology*, 3, 126–149.

Svavarsson, S. (2004) 'Pyrrho's Undecidable Nature', *Oxford Studies in Ancient Philosophy*, 27, 249–295.

Szaif, J. (2018) 'Socrates and the Benefits of Puzzlement', in Politis, V., & Karamanolis, G. E. (eds.) *The Aporetic Tradition in Ancient Philosophy*. Oxford: Oxford University Press, pp. 29–47.

Taylor, C. C. W. (1999) *The Atomists: Leucippus and Democritus*. Toronto: University of Toronto Press.

Teller, P. (2004) 'Discussion: What is a Stance?', *Philosophical Studies*, 121(2), 159–170.

Thorsrud, H. (2009) *Ancient Scepticism*. Stocksfield: Aucmen.

Turri, J. (2012) 'Pyrrhonian Skepticism Meets Speech-Act Theory', *International Journal for the Study of Skepticism*, 2(2), 83–98.

Vázquez, D. (2009) 'Reason in Check: the Skepticism of Sextus Empiricus', *Hermathena*, 186, 43–57.

(2019) 'The Systematic Use of the Five Modes for the Suspension of Judgement', *Manuscrito*, 42(3), 47–85.

(2020) 'The Stoics on the Education of Desire', in Bosch, M. (ed.) *Desire and Human Flourishing*. Cham: Springer, pp. 213–228.

(2021) 'Escepticismo radical y el alcance de los cinco tropos para la suspensión del juicio', in Ornelas, J. (ed.) *Rústicos versus Urbanos.* Mexico City: UNAM, pp. 95–108.

Wagner, V. (2021) 'Agnosticism as Settled Indecision', *Philosophical Studies*, 179, 671–697.

Wedgwood, R. (2002) 'The Aim of Belief', *Philosophical Perspectives*, 16, 267–297.

Whitmarsh, T. (2015) *Battling the Gods: Atheism in the Ancient World.* New York: Alfred A. Knopf.

Wieland, J. (2014) 'Sceptical Rationality', *Analytic Philosophy*, 55, 222–238.

Williams, M. (1996) *Unnatural Doubts*. Oxford: Blackwell.

(2004) 'The Agrippan Argument and Two Forms of Skepticism', in Sinnott-Armstrong, W. (ed.) *Pyrrhonian Skepticism*. New Mexico: Oxford University Press, pp. 121–145.

Woodruff, P. (1986) 'The Skeptical Side of Plato's Method', *Revue Internationale de Philosophie*, 40(156/157), 22–37.

(1988) 'Aporetic Pyrrhonism', *Oxford Studies in Ancient Philosophy*, 6, 139–168.

(2010) 'The Pyrrhonian Modes', in Bett, R. (ed.) *The Cambridge Companion to Ancient Scepticism*. Cambridge: Cambridge University Press, pp. 208–231.

Woolf, R. (2008) 'Socratic Authority', *Archiv für Geschichte der Philosophie*, 90(1), 1–38.

(2015) *Cicero: The Philosophy of a Roman Sceptic*. Abingdon: Routledge.

Zeller, E. (1909) *Die Philosophie Der Griechen in Ihrer Geschichtlichen Entwicklung*. Leipzig: Reislan.

Zinke, A. (2021) 'Rational Suspension', *Theoria*, 87(5), 1050–1066.

Acknowledgements

I am thankful to James Warren, who offered excellent feedback and was patient and understanding with the delays in my delivery of the final manuscript. I also owe a big thanks to the members of the Footnotes seminar, Vasilis Politis, John Dillon, audiences at King's College London and Trinity College Dublin, and an anonymous reviewer for feedback on preliminary drafts and presentations. As always, my biggest debt of gratitude goes to Gabriela Martínez Sainz for her unwavering support, encouragement, and help.

Cambridge Elements ≡

Ancient Philosophy

James Warren

University of Cambridge

James Warren is Professor of Ancient Philosophy at the University of Cambridge.
He is the author of *Epicurus and Democritean Ethics* (Cambridge, 2002), *Facing Death: Epicurus and his Critics* (2004), *Presocratics* (2007) and *The Pleasures of Reason in Plato, Aristotle and the Hellenistic Hedonists* (Cambridge, 2014). He is also the editor of *The Cambridge Companion to Epicurus* (Cambridge, 2009), and joint editor of *Authors and Authorities in Ancient Philosophy* (Cambridge, 2018).

About the Series

The Elements in Ancient Philosophy series deals with a wide variety of topics
and texts in ancient Greek and Roman philosophy, written by leading scholars in the field.
Taking a theme, question, or type of argument, some Elements explore it across antiquity
and beyond. Others look in detail at an ancient author, a specific work, or a part of
a longer work, considering its structure, content, and significance, or explore more
directly ancient perspectives on modern philosophical questions.

Cambridge Elements ≡

Ancient Philosophy

Elements in the Series

Printed in the United States
by Baker & Taylor Publisher Services